"Anne Peretz shares the approac[...] [...] own community in Burundi. Wha[...] has such a beautiful way of gettin[...] [...] uncomfortable issues and emerge with ho[...] [...]rective thinking. Her way of doing this is something that everyone can understand. The human connection found in *Opening Up* is visceral, eloquent, and beautifully redemptive. Anne Peretz's analysis of families' perils and their hopes should be required reading for anyone interested in the human condition."

—DEOGRATIAS NIYIZONKIZA,
subject of Tracy Kidder's *Strength in What Remains*

"*Opening Up* is not a book of facile guidelines or pat recipes. It's the beautifully told story of a set of journeys—the journeys of people struggling to stabilize their families, the journey of the trail-blazing organization The Parenting Journey, and the author's journey of lifelong learning, generosity, and openhearted dedication to the question 'what helps?' Essential reading for anyone interested in the helping professions."

—DOUG STONE,
author of *Difficult Conversations* and
Thanks for the Feedback

"Anne Peretz's book is taught in my Harvard Law classroom because it helps all people—students, parents, and advocates—to have meaningful conversations that teach empathic and intimate communications to resolve real and created crisis."

—CHARLIE NESSON,
William F. Weld, Professor of Law at Harvard Law School

"There is wisdom and insight, listening and witness, learning, serving, and helping in Anne Peretz's illuminating book. She challenges traditional therapeutic hierarchies that too often infantilize, pathologize, and disempower patients—particularly poor and marginalized patients living in underserved communities—by offering powerful narratives about the curiosity, generosity, mutual respect and reciprocity, dare we say love, that are at the heart of productive and dynamic therapeutic relationships. The family stories are at once painful and hopeful, courageous and vulnerable, exhausting and revelatory, filled with rage and anguish, discovery and laughter. They are particular stories that capture the universal human struggle; stories that bind us together in our quest for dignity and justice for families and children everywhere."

—Sara Lawrence-Lightfoot,
Emily Hargroves Fisher Research Professor of Education at
Harvard University and author of *Growing Each Other Up*

"Anne Peretz masterfully depicts families desperately in need of understanding and guidance. With vivid and compelling narratives, this book both educates and inspires the reader, showing where true hope is to be found in homes where we often see only despair."

—Jerome Groopman, MD,
Recanati Professor of Medicine at Harvard Medical School,
and author of *Anatomy of Hope*

Opening Up

The
Parenting
Journey

ANNE PERETZ

Radius Book Group
New York

Radius Book Group
A Division of Diversion Publishing Corp.
New York, NY
www.RadiusBookGroup.com

For more information, email info@radiusbookgroup.com.

First Hardcover edition: May 2021
First Trade Paperback edition: August 2022
Hardcover ISBN: 978-1-63576-761-2
Paperback ISBN: 978-1-63576-763-6
eBook ISBN: 978-1-63576-765-0

Library of Congress Control Number: 2020923221

Manufactured in the United States of America

10 9 8 7 6 5 4 3 2 1

Cover design by Tom Lau
Interior design by Neuwirth & Associates, Inc.

For my extraordinary and loving children, David, Lisa, Jesse, and Evgenia, who are continually teaching me how to be a better parent. They, and their nine progenies (Lucy, Henry, Freddy, Marley, Elias, Daphne, Arrow, Wilder, and Dusty) are my life.

Author's Note

THIS IS A BOOK ABOUT STORIES. IT IS NOT AN INSTRUCTION manual. For a brief overview of facilitator training and curricula, please see the appendix. For those interested in working with us or learning more about facilitator training, please go to https://parentingjourney.org.

The stories in this book are based on the stories of people who participated in or were involved with Parenting Journey at various times during the last 35 years and with whose help we have been shaped as an organization. To preserve their anonymity, all names and other identifying details have been changed.

Table of Contents

Foreword

MY LIFE HAS BEEN SHAPED BY THE GOOD FORTUNE OF BEING born into a family of storytellers. During his 97 years on earth, my father was known for his captivating, and often wickedly funny, stories. When my grandfather died in 1960, my father showed me my grandfather's scrapbooks, including the 1888 obituary of my great-great-grandmother Jane Gates. My career as a historian began that afternoon in 1960; I became obsessed with my family tree, and I began to shower my mother and father with questions for details about our ancestors. Eventually, my thirst for more of our literature and history led me to the study of what was then called Afro-American Studies, where I found the long and complex history of black men and women telling their own stories, both oral and written. In addition to an academic career focused on exploring the roots of the African American literary tradition, I have created historical documentaries as well as a series of genealogical films that explore the ancestry of Americans of all backgrounds. In all of these endeavors, I have witnessed the transformative value of storytelling.

In her concise and compelling book, *Opening Up*, Anne Peretz tells the fascinating story of the founding of her groundbreaking organization from its inception. In 1981, in Somerville,

Massachusetts, Peretz founded The Family Center to provide family therapy to at-risk, low-income families. Peretz and her team began with minimal resources, working out of their vehicles in order to provide free services to traumatized families within their homes in housing projects. Rather than label her clients with clinical diagnoses, Peretz's group has always focused on the strengths and resilience of families living under the enormous challenges of poverty and/or racial discrimination.

As the organization grew, The Family Center built a mental health clinic providing not just family and individual therapy but also community organization and health services. After 15 years of existence, their experiences led to the development of a therapeutic group, which they named Parenting Journey, an approach that builds on the "inherent strength in families" by recognizing the power of intergenerational relationships to effect change. By focusing on their own childhood experiences, the parent or caregiver is supplied the tools to rewrite their own narrative and improve their relationship with their children.

In 2014, Peretz renamed the central organization The Family Center to Parenting Journey as it expanded its reach outside of Massachusetts. Through its innovative and humane approach, Parenting Journey has become hugely successful, with over 500 locations in the United States and with satellites in Latin America and Africa. In its educational outreach, Parenting Journey trains facilitators to assist challenged families to retell their stories in life-changing ways.

Within the larger narrative structure of the history of Parenting Journey, Peretz forcefully makes the case for a fundamental shift in focus from traditional therapeutic modalities to open, respectful relationships between client and therapist, focusing on the commonalities of all family stories. *Opening Up* will be of special interest to those engaged in the caring professions, but Peretz's riveting stories of families under social and financial pressure will be of interest to all readers. To label these stories "case studies" would be a disservice to these beautifully crafted short narratives. Peretz is a natural storyteller, and her sensitivity and generosity mark each of these tales. In all of these stories, she stresses the importance of listening to and learning from those in need of assistance. While sensitively delineating the specifics of the struggles of her clients, Peretz eloquently emphasizes the universality of all families.

In *Opening Up*, Peretz expresses the hope that the lessons of her book will be of value to those seeking "to address the seemingly intractable knot of poverty, racism, violence, oppressions, stress, depression, and hopelessness that we face in our country and around the world." In 2020 in America, these endemic ills have combined with twin pandemics of racial unrest and COVID-19 to affect virtually every person and family. Now more than ever, Peretz's affirming stories offer much-needed hope and inspiration, an invaluable gift in these times.

Henry Louis Gates, Jr.
Alphonse Fletcher University Professor
Harvard University

Introduction

WALKING THROUGH THE SCRATCHED AND BATTERED STEEL door into Colleen's apartment felt like entering an abandoned prison. I was there because an unusual and inverted complaint had been lodged with the housing authority by Colleen against her two children for "parent abuse." My organization, a family therapy nonprofit called The Family Center, had been asked to follow up on this odd complaint.

Colleen was a 27-year-old white woman. Poor, and very overweight, she lived in a low-income housing development with her two children, 10-year-old Jimmy and 8-year-old Mara. Inside her apartment, I found myself amidst a tornado of toys, papers, old food, clothes, filthy bedding, and mattresses angled off the beds. In the middle of it all stood the perplexed mother, while her two pale children, their eyes glassy and bored, twitched as they fiddled with peanut butter sandwiches on the living room floor. The television was blaring, in competition with another equally loud TV in a different room.

Colleen started talking the moment I came in, even before I was all the way in the door. Without so much as a "how do you do," or any introductions at all, she began shouting at me about how the children were hitting her, yelling at her, and how they would not clean up the apartment. This was the "parent abuse" she had complained about.

I had expected to encounter an initial awkward silence, wariness, and a period where I would have to earn at least a modicum of trust before we could move ahead with the purpose—if there was one—for my visit. But this, like the complaint itself, was turned on its head. Colleen talked and talked. There was no room for me or the children to enter the conversation. Finally, we sat down. She talked, and I listened—until I stopped listening and just sat and watched television while she went on. The children were quiet. Were they perhaps interested in me? Maybe they saw me as a hope in what looked like a hopeless situation, or maybe I was just the next installment in a string of false hopes that had preceded me. Was I catching the disease, believing there was nothing that could be done here?

I thought to myself, "I should say something." Surely there was something to say. But there was nowhere to put in a sentence—the atmosphere was enveloped by Colleen talking and the television blaring. When a commercial came on—a man selling a vacuum cleaner—Colleen's attention turned to the screen, and she started talking back to the salesman as if he was her friend, a familiar figure with whom she was accustomed to having a dialogue. He asked, "Do you want your home to look like this?" pointing to a sparkling clean, freshly vacuumed room. "Yes," Colleen told him, she did. She didn't miss a beat. It was all one story, the salesman's story, her story, the story of her apartment and her children. It was the story of a woman completely overwhelmed with her life, unable to separate one thing from another, with nowhere to turn, and desperate to find her way out.

I couldn't find a thing to say that might reassure her. I had no strategy to offer her, no place to begin, not even a word of hope. I had been quickly and effectively inducted into the drama going on in Colleen's space, not knowing where to turn. I had never felt so helpless.

I left feeling like an absolute failure, thinking, "How did I get myself so quickly disabled in one short hour?" My first thought was, "I can't do this," even though at that point I didn't even know what "this" was. I wasn't a neophyte; I had a social work degree and a 12-year-old private family therapy practice. I had worked with troubled, overstressed, traumatized women before. I had conducted therapy groups. But with Colleen I felt like I was facing the first day of my social work field placement. I had to somehow find my voice and communicate hope to a desperate person needing to unload her burden without having the slightest sense that anyone could do anything about it. Hers wasn't so much a cry for help as it was just a cry.

My next visit started much as the first, but this time I was determined to engage the kids as well. Jimmy was a skinny little kid with hair sticking straight up, wearing a shirt that looked like he'd had it on all week. He was jumping nervously around, anticipating what I might say to him. Could this child really be a threat to his mother? He was guarded; it was hard to tell. Mara was even more guarded, looking sullenly down at her feet.

Colleen ordered Jimmy to clean up his room and gave him one garbage bag to do it. I wondered to myself what was supposed to go into the bag—garbage? Dirty clothes? Or things he might want to save? I suggested I'd go along to try to help him, but I didn't ask the critical question—what was the bag for? When we got into his room, there was the same chaos, a urine-smelling mattress and endless objects lying about—French fries mixed up with broken toys and pieces of clothing.

Without any prelude, Jimmy asked me to get into his closet with him. I had no idea why he wanted me in his closet. It seemed unrelated to cleaning up his room. But he was determined. We got in. The closet was very small, and it had no door. He scrunched down on one side, and I scrunched down on the other. I asked him if he was able to find things in his room. Did he know where everything was? Did he have an idea of how we could get started? We sat in there for a few moments in silence, then he said to me, "There are only two things I can't find." His tone was serious. I looked at his face. Then he said, "Love and friendship." What 10-year-old would say such a thing? Or could say such a thing? We stayed in the closet for a few more minutes. I put my hand on his. He was quiet.

When we got out of the closet and returned to Colleen, she demanded to know why Jimmy wasn't cleaning the room. She raised her voice; he began to shout back. I suggested to Colleen that maybe Jimmy was a little overwhelmed and needed a hug. She gave me a puzzled look. "Why should I give him a hug?" she said. "Nobody ever hugged me. He doesn't need a hug. I never hug him."

Jimmy was now at full throttle. I waited a few moments and tried again, "I think Jimmy might quiet down if I put him in a 'squeeze box'"—I had just made up the term. I threw my arms around him in a pretty strong clench intended to look to Colleen like a kind of punishing restraint, but which felt to Jimmy like, well, a hug. He calmed right down.

In my next visit, with some reluctance, Colleen learned how to use the "squeeze box." At first, she looked extremely awkward, but eventually both she and Jimmy seemed able to do it pretty well. Colleen wasn't ready for the soft emotional feelings of a gentle hug, but she could understand power and control and a strong, restrictive embrace. It was a start. Maybe we could build on it. As I walked out of the projects that day, I knew that this was going to be my life's work—taking a different approach, finding what is working in the family, and amplifying it with exercises and interventions which provide hope and possibility.

Colleen's family was one of our first client families at The Family Center. Our organization, which began in Somerville, Massachusetts, in 1981, was created to offer family therapy services to low-income communities, especially to families like Colleen's. In one of the housing developments we worked in, a researcher had once asked a group of children like Jimmy and Mara where they thought they would be in 10 years. By 20, the boys said that they thought they would be dead. The girls said they thought they would be pregnant.

When we started, there was so much my colleagues and I didn't know about helping families with such high levels of trauma, but we wanted to learn. Over 15 years, we created a mental health clinic that included individual and family therapy groups, as well as community-wide activities such as children's fashion shows designed by mothers, preventive health services such as women's mammograms and flu shots, a community soap opera, and help with organizing in the community to get more services.

From these experiences, we developed a therapeutic group program called Parenting Journey that encompassed lessons learned in our first 15 years working in housing projects. Because the Parenting Journey program could be taught to others and could expand our reach—including being developed in other cities, states, and countries—it became the major focus of our organization. As Parenting Journey became known outside of Massachusetts, we renamed our entire organization Parenting Journey in 2014.

Parenting Journey has created an evidence-based therapeutic program whose focus is on building on the strengths inherent in families, with a particular emphasis on intergenerational relationships and patterns. Many parents and caregivers are often best served by first taking a step back and reflecting on experiences from their own childhoods before they begin to develop concrete goals for improving their relationships with their children. Our five program iterations—Parenting Journey I, Parenting Journey II, Parents in Recovery, Parenting Journey for Fathers, and Parenting in America—have now been replicated in over 500 locations throughout the United States, with some also underway in Latin America and Africa. Along with these five programs for parents, we also offer training for group facilitators. This book focuses on the development of our core program, Parenting Journey I, which has been the basis of the common threads that run throughout all of our programs.

At Parenting Journey, we try to shift the common helping professions' perspective—especially for families living in poverty and affected by the virulent effects of racism—away from a concentration on deficits and diagnoses, toward the strengths and resilience that inhere in every struggling family. We believe that all parents deserve respect, and that families have abilities and strengths that often go unrecognized even by the families themselves. Our work is to help undo years, sometimes generations, of painful discrimination and mistreatment, deeply internalized, and to underscore these strengths and to support their effectiveness. It is about hope and possibility, about turning around negative patterns and self-regard, even reversing damaging effects on the brain. And yes, these damaging neural patterns can be reversed! They can be reversed by the loving, attuned attention of parents to their children and to themselves.

Above all, the Parenting Journey is about helping parents understand themselves and their children, and helping them to strengthen the bonds that tie them to each other. Our focus is on giving families hope that they, from one generation to the next, can move forward toward joy and well-being, and by doing so, they will build strong communities.

This book, *Opening Up,* tells our organization's story from its early days as The Family Center to our place in the world today as Parenting Journey and our hopes for the future. It tells the story of how our core program, Parenting Journey I, developed, and it also tells the stories of brave and challenged families like Colleen's from low-income neighborhoods who have encountered the toxic intergenerational stressors of their surroundings, family histories, systemic inequalities, and internal pain, and who have struggled to get beyond them.

These stories are about how families thrive, how they get into trouble, and how their often-unrecognized strengths can enable them to overcome even severe difficulties and trauma. *Opening*

Up is also about communities, and how they can be supportive or destructive in the lives of children and families. It is about how external pressures resonate internally, creating stress, fear, and a sense of hopelessness, and how these characteristics can get transmitted down the line. And it is also about how, with the right help, the downward spiral can be interrupted, and how even severely traumatized families can regain stability and hope. It is about how these families become leaders in their communities, combatting institutionalized racism, sexism, and degradation.

Parenting is perhaps the most difficult, demanding, and important job in the world. The challenge of raising children to be successful adults and good parents in their own right is a universal one. This book does not espouse a "right way" to raise a child, but it does identify qualities that tend to be universally effective and others that are not.

My hope is that this book will help shape attitudes and social policies that contribute to family successes, and not to a continuation of the downward spiral parents and children may be on, which is often assisted inadvertently by negative and even punitive practices. This book is for practitioners, clinicians, social workers, parent educators, people running government programs, human service nonprofits, policy makers, as well as the ordinary interested reader. Perhaps it will help policy makers direct their attention to strengthening parent-child relationships rather than the current very expensive and destructive emphasis on substitute parenting and out-of-home care. These are necessary in some cases, to be sure, but they should not be a knee-jerk reaction to pain and suffering.

At its heart, this book is about how vulnerable people can be helped to heal so that they can be functional adults, compassionate, attuned parents, and active members of their community. Most especially, it is a plea to think differently about families. It is a plea to develop a perspective that searches out the strengths and resilience in individuals and families, and does not regard families, especially families living in poverty and members of minority groups, from a point of view of deficit, with psychiatric diagnoses dictating programs of change. My hope is that others may find value in Parenting Journey's experiences and approach in order to address the seemingly intractable knot of poverty, racism, violence, oppression, stress, depression, and hopelessness that we face in our country and around the world.

1

MEETING FAMILIES

Billy is on the Roof, Joey is Hungry, Mia is Hiding

BILLY

Billy was up on the roof of his school, threatening to jump. Police and firemen arrived, ladders were raised, and a net was put in place. Kids in the street were laughing, taunting him, encouraging him, admiring him. They wanted to see him jump. Some were scared, some teary, some possibly envious. This was not a normal school day.

After the incident, his school referred him to a therapist at a local hospital for individual therapy. The therapist didn't know much about Billy when they started. Billy was African American, 13 years old, not particularly good at school, and, like most of his friends, kind of a goof-off. He liked to wear baggy pants and long, colored shirts and cut his hair short in the popular flat-top style. He could be boisterous, but recently he had become glum and distracted, sitting at his desk and staring into space. He had also been experiencing fits of anger, picking fights and swearing at friends, even at teachers. The therapist diagnosed him as suffering from bipolar disorder.

Billy resisted going to his therapy sessions, and when he did go, he didn't seem to be benefiting from them. His therapist said he was not forthcoming or willing to talk about his family or how he was feeling. The therapy appeared to be going nowhere.

It just so happened that at the time, Billy's 10-year-old sister Isa was in one of our girls' therapy groups at The Family Center. Their mother, Vicky, suggested that maybe Billy could see a therapist with us. Isa told him it was a nice place. The therapist at the hospital agreed to give it a try.

A meeting was arranged for Billy with Crystal, a Family Center therapist, who asked that the whole family come for an initial session before anything else was done. Since Isa was already in one of our groups, and Vicky was peripherally involved in her daughter's group, seeing the entire family first made sense to everyone. So, Vicky brought her four children—Billy, Isa, 8-year-old Latasha, and baby Tonya—to The Family Center to meet with Crystal and the leader of Isa's girls' group, Daphne.

Crystal began the session by asking everyone in the family to take turns making a picture of how they saw their family. She explained that instead of using paper and pencils, everyone would agree to be a piece of clay that could be molded by a "sculptor." Each family member would take a turn at being the sculptor who would use the other family members as the raw materials to create the picture.

Crystal explained that there were three rules to making this sculpture: vertical distance—who was higher than whom—would show power; horizontal distance—who was closest to whom—would show emotional closeness; and facial expressions and gestures with arms and legs and the whole body would express the type of emotion felt. The "sculptor" could arrange the other members of the family any way he or she wanted. In this way, they could all see how each of them viewed the family from the perspectives of who was the most and least powerful, who was close to whom and who more distant, and what the emotional quality of each relationship was. The family was intrigued by this novel game and was willing to participate. Billy agreed to go first.

Crystal asked Billy to place his family members in relation to each other according to these rules in a way that best expressed how he understood and saw his family, and lastly, to place himself in the picture as well. She also gave him a life-sized doll that he could use to represent anyone outside the family whom he thought might be important to the picture.

Billy started with his mother, deciding to build the sculpture around her. He had her sit on a chair. He placed baby Tonya next to her on her right side. He asked his mother to smile as a gesture of love toward the baby. He placed Latasha at some distance behind his mother and to her left. Asked what her expression or gesture was, he said she was looking away from the family. He also placed Isa on the left, but close to Vicky, with only a little space between them. Her expression was sadness, with her head bowed.

Crystal asked Billy if they all held the same amount of power in the family since they were all positioned at about the same height. Billy thought carefully, and had his mother stand. Then he changed his mind and had her sit down again. He put Latasha on her knees on the floor, lower than Vicky. He also had Isa sit on the floor, still with a sad, resigned expression. He had her cross her arms in front of her. When Crystal asked him to place himself in the picture, Billy put himself closest to his sisters, but a long distance away and standing. His expression was angry.

When Crystal encouraged him to show more of that anger, Billy put up his fists in a kind of helpless gesture. Then Crystal asked him if anyone was missing. He got up, dragged a chair over to his mother, and then grabbed the life-sized doll and stuffed it on the chair between his mother and Isa, so that the doll was hovering above the two of them. He said this was his mother's boyfriend. He was clearly agitated by this time, so Crystal deviated from her original plan and asked the question she had been saving for after she had seen everyone's picture. She waited for Billy to get into his position behind his sisters, and then she asked him, "Billy, can you now show us a picture of how you would like your family to be?" He leapt forward, grabbed the doll, and threw it on the floor and started pummeling it, screaming at it with almost animal sounds.

After this, the other family members, who were clearly shaken by Billy's performance, made rather innocuous, calcified family sculptures. There was very little distinction between their depictions of the existing family dynamic and what was desired. They were covering something up and fearful—frozen by Billy's revelation of an unspoken family secret. Isa looked particularly scared and upset.

Seeing Isa's response, Crystal told the family that she, Vicky, Isa, and Daphne would meet the following day, and then the whole family would have a meeting in the afternoon afterward.

The next day, Isa was afraid to talk, but Daphne and Crystal slowly helped her to tell her story. It came out that she was being sexually abused by Vicky's boyfriend. Isa was terrified of the boyfriend, who had threatened to kill her if she told anyone, and she was scared that her mother might not believe her and might be angry at her for telling her story. The two therapists promised to protect Isa from the boyfriend. They told her that they would report the incident to the Department of Social Services (DSS), which would probably have the man arrested. Then they helped her have a conversation with her mother.

Vicky *was* angry at Isa. She didn't want to believe her, and told everyone in the room it wasn't true. Isa's knuckles were digging into a pillow on the couch. She looked away, tears dripping down her face. Crystal said to Vicky, "Look at your daughter. Do you think she's making this up?" Vicky glanced at Isa and looked away again. "No," Crystal said, "LOOK at your daughter. What do you see? Do you see someone lying? Or do you see someone suffering and scared and not being cared for by her mother?" "Well," Vicky said meekly, "I didn't know." Crystal went and sat next to Vicky as a comforting gesture, saying, "I'm at your side," but she didn't let her off the hook. She was challenging her from close up. Isa got off the couch and ran to Daphne, who hugged her and took her on her lap.

As a family therapy clinic, we needed to take several actions immediately. First, we were obligated by law to report this incident to the DSS. There were two ways this could be done. We could file the incident ourselves, which had to be done within 24 hours and had the greatest risk of the family being separated. Or, we could "partially" report the incident and ask for five additional days during which Vicky could file the incident herself and tell the entire story. We strongly preferred doing it this way because it would avoid pitting us against her, while also encouraging her to be a strong, protective mother for her children.

A great fear for a lot of children like Billy and his siblings who live in the projects is that when something like this happens—a child being abused—the child will be removed from the family and taken into a foster home for safety. This is a dreaded possibility for many of these kids, even if they may be in rough straits at home. Department of Social Services safety workers who remove a child from home to avoid a repeat assault often underestimate the emotional trauma caused by separating the child from his or her family. Separations of this sort add enormous additional loss and pain to the abuse the child is already suffering from.

We discussed this up front with Vicky and said that we hoped that she would call the DSS herself to report what had happened. If the call came from a concerned parent trying to protect her children, she was more likely to be allowed to keep all of her kids at home. After a day or so, she agreed to report the incident herself.

The second necessity following our meeting with Vicky and Isa was to get the boyfriend permanently out of the house and make sure he couldn't decide to come back in the middle of the night. The police issued a restraining order and assured Vicky that they meant business.

After this, we returned to focusing on getting the whole family back together to address Billy's feelings and behavior, as well as reassuring the family that they would not be separated as a protective measure by the DSS. We were afraid Billy might not show up, but he did. He was silently treated as a sort of hero. He had shown all of us, his family and the therapists, what was really going on in his family. Crystal asked him if he thought that holding this information inside of himself had anything to do with what had happened in school. Billy nodded his head. How long had he known about what was going on between Isa and the boyfriend? He was quiet for a long time before he eventually spoke up. He said he had found out just a short time ago, and by accident. He had seen the boyfriend and Isa together. He didn't want to talk about it and began pacing around the room. Did he feel relieved? "Yes," he said. Then "No," he felt scared. Crystal explained to him everything that was going to happen next. The police would keep the boyfriend away, and Billy's family was going to figure things out together.

With the crisis identified and the immediate needs dealt with, we were able to start meeting with the family to help them strengthen their family bonds and try to advance their well-being. The children were very relieved. We were not immediately worried about Billy, though we still had plans to get back to him and why he had been on the roof. That had been a pretty extreme way of making a statement or a cry for help. We thought there was probably more to it.

In the meetings that followed, Billy's story emerged in a way it hadn't with his first therapist. Billy was a vulnerable kid, wanting to find a safe place, with a family he could trust, which he was not finding at home. As a result, he was ideal prey for the youth gangs who were prowling his neighborhood.

He had been approached by some slightly older boys who asked him to join them. They were well known in the neighborhood as trouble. Billy wanted to belong to something, but he did not really want to join a gang. He just wanted a good friend whose family he might be able to go home to. But the older boys were persistent, and he felt trapped, caught between his family, where he could not tell the truth and protect his sister, and the gang, which was both tempting and intimidating. One day things finally came to a head. A boy from the gang told him that he was either with them or against them. He had to decide that day. Billy's response was to go up on the roof and threaten to jump off.

As we can see from this story, "symptoms" mean different things depending on where one focuses. Symptoms are signs of distress, and in this case, the startling, attention-getting symptom was Billy threatening to jump off the roof. But what was it a symptom of? A bipolar disorder? A signal to the world that his family was in trouble and needed help? A cry for help in a community where he was trapped between two bad choices?

How we understand the meaning of the symptom will prescribe what line of intervention to take. And how we see the symptom will depend on where we choose to look. It is not necessarily an either/or situation, but if one approach is emphasized and another overlooked—which is often the case in the helping professions—we may hit a wall, or we may miss something terribly wrong that needs attention.

Billy and his family were among some of the early clients of The Family Center, coming to us around the time that we were starting to develop the first exploratory Parenting Journey group, which laid the bedrock for later Parenting Journey programs. Going into the first family meeting with Billy and his family, no one thought that the real "patients," to use a medical term, would be Isa and her mother. In this kind of situation, family therapists would say that Billy was the "identified patient," meaning that he was the one showing the symptoms, but not necessarily the one who needed the most help. In fact, it is often the strongest member of the family who raises the red flag.

In this case, once we had met with the entire family, it became immediately obvious that it was not Billy who needed individual attention as long as his family situation was addressed. We continued to work with the family through the resolution of the issues brought up in the illuminating session with Vicky and Isa, and, in part, because Vicky had decided to call the DSS herself to report the abuse of her daughter, the DSS did ultimately decide to keep the family together.

As the situation was addressed over time, Billy regained his earlier enthusiasm and goofiness, and Isa started on the long road to living as a survivor, now with the support and understanding of her family. Vicky eventually became a member of our very first Parenting Journey group, where she could get the kinds of support she needed to accept and deal with the immense challenges she faced in her life, including both her own personal interests and those of her children.

CHARMAINE

Charmaine enjoyed expressing herself with her clothing, dressing in tight skirts and tops that she knew looked good on her, doing her hair in complicated twists, and wearing high heels before they were fashionable. She was 31, and African American. She had an on-and-off part-time job at the local hardware store, which she had trouble holding onto. She was a good worker but was very sensitive to criticism from her bosses. When criticized, she'd react with an angry epithet, which would often get her fired. Although she hadn't come to recognize it yet, her fear of being fired and her sense of its looming inevitability would trigger her angry outbursts, which would result in the very outcome that she feared. This was a pattern that she struggled with not just in the hardware store but in other jobs as well.

Charmaine had six children, with four different fathers, none of whom were very involved in helping her take care of the kids. And while she had many friends, handling all of her children was a constant challenge for her. To cope with the stresses of her life, she would frequently get high, and didn't always manage to bring enough food into the house. One day her eldest child, 12-year-old Joey, finding nothing to eat in the apartment, called the DSS and told them he was hungry. When the department representative knocked on their door, Charmaine shut it in the woman's face and told her to get lost.

With his phone call, Joey had exposed the family to the "system," which opened a way for the state to intervene in the family's affairs. At the time, Charmaine's children were enrolled in The Family Center's after-school groups, and now, with the state's intervention, we found ourselves working with Charmaine as well.

Everyone involved knew the family dance. Trouble would often start with one of Charmaine's current boyfriends or with a past partner. She would try to use this person to obtain drugs, would ask him to give her money for the kids, or would seek help from him in other ways. But instead of her using them, the men mostly took advantage of her, showing up on the day her welfare check arrived in the mail, when there was sure to be food in the house. The most frequent of these visitors was Joey Sr., who we came to suspect might be sexually assaulting one of Charmaine's daughters, 9-year-old Mia. Charmaine told us that whenever he came over, Mia cried uncontrollably and tried to hide in her room, refusing to speak to her mother or anyone else.

Charmaine knew what was really going on, but she felt too powerless to do anything about it. She would allow situations to develop where Joey Sr. and Mia were alone in the house, either neglectfully, or by being "too busy" to stay at home. She pretended not to see what was happening.

One day, in an emotional therapy session at The Family Center, Charmaine confided in us she had been sexually molested when she was Mia's age. She said that she felt paralyzed at the time, with no one protecting her, and now, seeing the scene repeating itself in front of her with her daughter, she felt paralyzed again and emotionally numb. Instead of being able to express these deeper emotions with Mia, she acted toward her daughter with bursts of unexplained anger. So not only was Mia the object of repeated sexual abuse, but she was also the object of her mother's rage, without knowing why her mother was behaving this way toward her.

Charmaine and Mia were continuing to have difficulty addressing the pain and toxicity of the situation, until one afternoon when one of our therapists asked them to try an exercise where they sat across the table from each other and pretended they were looking into a mirror. Mia was more than willing, while Charmaine, muttering an obscenity, balked at taking the challenge. She was angry at being asked to waste her time on such a stupid exercise. When she finally raised her head and looked at her daughter, she was taken aback. She looked harder. What she saw were her own slightly frightened brown eyes, her own crooked mouth, the little separation between her front teeth, and the same curls framing her face that were looking for somewhere to go. And then she began to cry.

Seeing herself in her daughter in this way was such a shock that Charmaine began to open up right there in the session. She and Mia began a painful conversation in which, for the first time, Charmaine told Mia something about what had happened to her when she was a child. Tears came from Mia's eyes as her mother reached through the imaginary mirror to hold her daughter's arms in a tight embrace, the gesture telling Mia what she needed to know about her mother's feelings for her.

With Mia still in the room, the therapist worked with Charmaine to understand why she felt as helpless in protecting her daughter as she had been in defending herself. Through this process, Mia, though still angry and fearful at moments, learned something about her mother that brought them together. One large result from this conversation was that Joey Sr. was no longer allowed in the house.

The stories that Charmaine told her daughter and the therapist about her own history with sexual assault were heartbreaking. She had been raised in four different foster families, and was regularly raped by either the father or the male siblings in each family. As a child and an adolescent, she was moved between foster homes because she was "hard to handle," and there was frequently an aura of blame ascribed to her by the social service agency for being difficult. Her mother had been a drug user who had been depressed from the day Charmaine was born. Her mother had wanted to get her back but had never become stable enough to do so. Charmaine longed for the mother she never had, and carried that longing from her childhood into her adulthood.

She had survived all of this, and she came to realize that now as an adult, the awareness of the abuse, the lack of love, protection, and caretaking had become a dim fact in the back of her mind. She had relegated it to a past that she did her best to shut out, denying it had any relevance to her current life, over which she felt she had some control. But however she thought about it, or didn't think about it, the past was a latent reality that obstructed her desire to be the kind of mother she wanted to be. This childhood experience of a complete lack of security and support also showed up in her interpretation of workplace rejections, and played a large role in triggering the fear and rage that cost her job after job.

Charmaine's youthful experiences haunted her, and she was now paying the price a second time, as the same abuses rippled over to her own children. We feared that without serious intervention at a number of levels, the family might remain caught in a cycle of abusive situations that could go on for generations.

Slowly, and over time, looking back made looking forward more possible. Charmaine worked on "making sense" of her life, and by so doing, she opened her "window of tolerance" for holding the past in perspective while living more actively and affectively in the present. Her children began to thrive, she controlled her drug use, and Joey Jr. ended up in a boarding school—a smart boy with good grades.

But even with all of the positive changes, Charmaine remained vulnerable to being held hostage by inappropriate and sometimes dangerous men, and her choices of male companions continued to affect her children as they grew into maturity. As a young man, Joey Jr. at one point acquired a gun with the intention of threatening one of Charmaine's boyfriends, whom he called a "mother molester." No actual violence took place, but the extremity of Joey's actions was a chilling reminder of how hard it can be to break such traumatic cycles of anger and abuse.

2

THE FAMILY CENTER

Telephones in the Bathroom

I FOUNDED THE FAMILY CENTER WITH MY TEACHER AND fellow family therapist, David Kantor, in 1981. Our core belief was that when a baby is born, all parents intend and hope to be the best parents they are capable of being. Our goal was to help our client families fulfill that intention, even in the face of the severe personal challenges and life circumstances they were facing. I had a persistent faith that even our most stressed families had inner strengths they could use to understand themselves better and be the parents they wanted to be, if only they could find those strengths. Our job was to help the families do that, then help them build on it. I thought of this approach as in some ways similar to Michelangelo's view of sculpting—chipping away at the hard stone to reveal the powerful figure underneath.

Kantor had been my teacher at The Family Institute of Cambridge, where he helped open my eyes to the centrality of family in the therapeutic process. One of the important figures in family therapy, he was a hugely creative individual who developed many family therapy concepts and wrote various groundbreaking articles and books, including *Inside the Family*. At Harvard, Tufts, and his own institutes, he taught students and trained many therapists over a long lifetime of teaching. A brilliant original thinker, he also had an off-kilter humorous side. For years he ran a one-day-a-week mobile bookstand—"the World's 100 Best Books"—pulled by Jenny the Donkey near Harvard Square. His theory, called structural-analytic psychotherapy, appealed to me when I was a student trying to find ways to materialize ideas I had about working with poor and underserved families.

In the beginning, our clinical team was very small. The day-to-day running of our operation, and especially our work with our clients, came down to just myself, two other clinical staff members, and an administrator. Kantor meanwhile was developing the Kantor Family Institute (KFI), training therapists with the thought that some of the trainees at KFI would become interns at the Family Center, thus providing free service to low-income families living in two public housing projects.

At first, our clinical staff worked out of our vehicles, a 1972 Chevy and a 1976 Plymouth truck, parking in front of the housing projects and using them as our offices. Then we found a former boarding house, which was functional, even if it didn't necessarily meet all the required standards for getting a mental health license. The main impediment to our getting a license, once we were fully in business, was that we had put telephones in the bathrooms. Since we didn't need all of the unit's bathrooms but did require more office space, we put shelves on tubs and used toilet seats as chairs for staff to use for telephone interviews. We were a seat-of-your-pants operation, eager to get started. Kantor hated being constrained by rules even more than I did. We happily improvised and made do with what we had.

We understood that to be effective in our work, we needed to learn from the families. We needed to join with them in a collaborative effort. We knew that traditional parenting education classes, even when they were available, didn't hit the mark. Without understanding the deep effects of trauma induced primarily by the combined results of generations of racism, poverty, and violence (in those days we knew much less about trauma than we do today), and which virtually every one of our parents had experienced in one form or another, being told by a privileged person (who was usually middle class and white) what to do with your child just didn't fly. There were too many untouched issues getting in the way.

In the housing projects where we worked, we asked questions and listened carefully. Our clients were our teachers, and they knew it. Reciprocity was one of our core principles. We learned from them in order to help, and we traded concrete skills, for example, helping someone bring home groceries in one of our vehicles in exchange for a Spanish lesson. We were curious, not judgmental. We were respectful. And we were appreciative. Colleen once brought me a five-pound chunk of cheese she had picked up at the food pantry. I was touched. It was an important gift.

It didn't take long to understand some of the underlying facts of life that many of our clients were dealing with. We saw the effects of blatant racism—not only in the inability to get good jobs, to go to good schools, but in the pervasive sense that if you were black or brown, there was something innately inferior about you. We learned of the pervasiveness of abuse. We learned that people tended to be unaware of the lasting significance of what they were carrying with them and how this was affecting their lives, and also how their experiences might carry over into the next generation. We learned that they were, often out of necessity, stuck in rigid patterns, fearful of change and manifesting their fears in angry terms. When a painful issue came up, it often led to angry shouting. We learned that many had lost hope and couldn't even visualize a different life. They were better at visualizing death. We saw that without a loving adult in their lives (usually their mother), children felt chronically unsafe. But we also understood that even if a mother was abusing her child, underneath it all, she *wanted* to be a good parent. Too much had gotten in the way between giving birth and her ongoing struggles, so that "being the best mom" had disappeared from sight.

My own interest in pursuing family therapy began with the circumstances of my childhood and continued with my experiences as a young adult. I was a child of privilege and, with my mother's death, when I was six, also a child of loss. I was told that she had been a remarkably compassionate person, and while I don't remember her well, I do know that my mother's hero, Eleanor Roosevelt, stood for her as someone who cared deeply about helping people suffering from poverty.

My parents had met volunteering at the Lenox Hill Settlement House in New York City. My father later worked for the State

Department and for the United Nations. He was a dedicated public servant with a career ranging from the reconstruction of Europe after World War II, where he ran the Marshall Plan in Paris, to administering the United Nations Relief and Works Agency for Palestine Refugees after the Israeli War for Independence, where he was responsible for resettling or caring for almost a million Arab refugees. This kind of work was his passion.

When I was 14 and 15 years old, my father took me along on some of his working visits to the refugee camps. There, I experienced the generosity of impoverished people living on the edge, the difficulties of developing trusting relationships with them, and the rumors that spread about the malevolent intent of the very UN organizations that were trying to bring some relief to their suffering. I felt the power of those visits deeply. In retrospect, they gave me an advanced taste of some of the experiences I would have later, working with families at Parenting Journey.

I remember two conflicting aspects of the refugees' lives that particularly struck me. One was the hardship and poverty of families living in torn tents, with mud floors, with no access to water except at the local well from which women carried the daily supply on their heads, no electricity, and no sanitation facilities. The other was the deep cynicism on the part of local Palestinian leaders who prevented the simplest improvements in daily life—such as digging latrines or replacing tents with cinderblock houses—in order to maintain intense misery for the greater goal of keeping the dream alive of returning to their homes in Palestine. What the UN built during the day, the Palestinian leadership often destroyed at night.

Yet, along with the misery in the camps, and the political passion of community leaders trying to keep the fervor of returning home burning, generosity and love of family were also clearly present. Both sides—the ordinary people and their leaders—had their priorities. They were all stakeholders in a bad situation, and from their different perspectives, they had different solutions. This was a lesson I learned early, even though I wasn't sure what to make of it at the time.

As a young teenager, just before my father began taking me to the camps, I had started rebelling against the authorities in my life. We were living in Paris, where I was enrolled in a French school, which I hated. I hated the rote memory way of teaching and learning, and I hated the confining rules. I began cutting school to hang out at a local arcade or with friends who were going to the American school. One day I lit my desk on fire, which accomplished the goal of getting me expelled. This incident helped contribute to my later professional belief that "symptomatic behavior" is not necessarily a sign of pathology, but rather it can be a metaphoric creation that calls attention to what needs attending.

As I grew older, my political interests began to take shape. My time in the Middle East, witnessing the refugee camps, had already influenced these interests, and they were further impacted by other events going on in the world. I found in the developing civil rights movement in the late 1950s and the protests against the Vietnam War in the 1960s a growing passion for justice.

In the early 1960s, I was living on a U.S. Air Force base in the Philippines with my first husband. He was a doctor who was paying back his medical school tuition to the U.S. Air Force. We had a front-row seat to the beginnings of the Vietnam War long before it was officially recognized. I considered the war to be a great mistake, and seen up close, it was even worse than we

had imagined in 1961 at the first anti-war march on the White
House.

There was no doubt about the causes that inflamed me, yet I
wasn't clear on how I wanted to participate. I joined demonstra-
tions and volunteered for political groups. I became a community
organizer with the National Welfare Rights Organization and a
union organizer with hospital workers. Still unclear about the
best way to make a difference, and feeling that we were often tilt-
ing at windmills, I completed a social work degree with the intent
of delving more deeply into what was making all kinds of people
behave in somewhat destructive ways and whether there was a
better solution to the challenges of the times. At the National
Welfare Rights marches, it felt like we were missing something.
It seemed to me that marches didn't contribute to lasting change.
While they may have provided some a slight monetary improvement—they didn't seem to do much to actually strengthen or ease
parents' basic circumstances.

Over time, I felt myself more and more drawn to working
with families facing incapacitating systemic challenges. I became
committed to finding a more effective way of supporting these
families. While I was working as a therapist with my own private
practice, I also volunteered with a housing project where I could
work with low-income and challenged people and learn from
them.

Years before, as a student, I had interned at a progressive
agency where, surprisingly, the counseling services were traditional psychodynamic one-on-one sessions. During my time
there, I noticed that mothers coming into sessions by themselves
to be counseled by a well-meaning therapist about their feelings and past histories wasn't proving effective. The mother was

usually emotionally exhausted. She felt she was being blamed for her situation, whether the feeling was valid or not, and after several sessions with a counselor she usually felt no more hopeful than when she first came in.

Typically, the client was a mother with several children, living in a chaotic situation. There might be violence in the home, addiction, a chronically ill family member, lead paint flaking off the walls, unhealthy or insufficient food, or any variety of other stressors. As I was observing or participating in these sessions, I was asking myself a simple question: what was most important to this woman? And the answer was obvious—her family. I thought, why not see the whole family together and try to figure out from a wider angle what was going on that was so stressful to this mother? And from there see how the family might share the burden or at least make some small changes to lighten the mother's load?

This idea, along with two others, was percolating in the back of my mind. I knew it would be difficult to get entire families to come into a clinic, so the obvious thing to do would be to go to their homes. I also knew that if the mother felt blamed, she would probably also feel hopeless and defensive and even hostile to this intrusion, so the approach had to be positive, helping the family see its strengths and abilities instead of focusing on their weaknesses. These three ideas formed the bedrock of The Family Center: working with the whole family instead of just an individual, going to clients' homes instead of insisting they come to a clinic, and looking for strengths instead of problems. This was a framework for assisting people who suffered unbelievable stress and often generations of inherited pain.

There are many things that can contribute to the attitudes that we bring to our lives and our work, and sometimes they can come from unexpected sources. While I was growing up, I had favorite childhood books and characters, as everyone does, and as I began my professional life, I noticed that some of my childhood favorites seemed to resonate with my experiences at work. As a child, I had been fascinated by Dorothy and the Wizard of Oz. As time went on and I became a family therapist, Dorothy and the Wizard seemed to me the prototype of a cotherapy team. Each had skills and influence, and each was dependent on the other for success. Dorothy often seemed not to know where she was or what she was doing—she had a kind of innocent, bewildered, but hopeful look about her. At the same time, she seemed to instinctively know the right thing to do. In the story, she listens to the complaints and longings of the Scarecrow, the Cowardly Lion, and the Tin Woodman. She doesn't challenge them on their perceptions of themselves; instead, she treats them as she sees them—wise, brave, and full of feeling. They live up to her expectations, even as they are largely unaware of their abilities and see themselves in a more negative light. They don't believe she can give them what they think they need, even as she treats them respectfully; after all, she's just a girl trying to get home. They think they need magical confirmation from the powerful Wizard. The Wizard can make complete what Dorothy began.

As I continued as a therapist, I found that being in cotherapy situations was quite like that. Sometimes I was Dorothy, sometimes I was the Wizard. This theme of multiple perspectives eventually led my coworkers and me at The Family Center to a view that partnership was valuable in the therapy process. We often need more than just ourselves to make a real difference and to reveal the qualities our clients have hidden inside themselves. Sometimes the necessary partner is a cotherapist, sometimes a family member or close friend of our clients, sometimes the families themselves. As a friend and mentor of mine, Eileen Brown, the founder of Cambridge College, would often say, "Not any one of us knows what all of us know."

Another character who resonated with me as a child was the TV detective Columbo, played by Peter Falk. Columbo was a bumbling police investigator who didn't seem to know what he was doing, but, as you watched him, you realized that even though he made mistakes in some of his assumptions (and sometimes on purpose!), something always led him to the place he needed to be in order to solve a crime. You couldn't be certain that his solution was going to work. You weren't even quite sure that he was the one in charge. He surely was not Sherlock Holmes, with a confident sense that he could solve any mystery. But with all his apparent confusion and lack of clarity, Columbo did make progress, and he did end up figuring things out—not that different from a therapist's relation to the deep and complex problems of families in trouble. The therapist often faces these problems through a fog of tentativeness and unsureness, which only unravel themselves with searching coupled with humility.

As I trained and began thinking about the characteristics of various therapeutic styles, I realized that I was predisposed toward a side-by-side approach and an attitude of, "Let's explore this together." I had neither the inclination nor the confidence to know what was right all by myself. The Family Center had elements of this perspective embedded in its model, which Parenting Journey continues today.

A third childhood favorite was Curious George. Curious George was always into things, wanting to understand and have fun. He was rarely punished, and the Man with the Yellow Hat always appreciated him. Curious George had good intentions but broke a few things along the way. Playfulness, risk-taking, and acceptance of mistakes all became part of the therapeutic environment of Parenting Journey. Curious George wasn't a bad model for that process. By my good fortune, Margret Rey, who wrote and illustrated *Curious George* together with her husband, lived near me in Cambridge and became a friend of mine and also a friend to Parenting Journey. Today, in the waiting room of our Somerville, Massachusetts, clinic, we have paintings and pictures of Curious George and *Curious George* books and toys. The room was a dying gift from Margret Rey. The books and pictures and toys offer a subliminal, distinctly positive message for the children who come in with their parents.

ESTELLE

Around the time that The Family Center was getting close to being launched, I met a woman named Estelle.

Estelle was a welfare organizer who was working part time for John, a friend and former boss of mine. One day, John called me. Estelle had had a breakdown of some sort. She had been hospitalized in a local psychiatric ward, from where she had called him, terrified. He asked if I could visit her, see what her condition was, and possibly get her out.

I went to the hospital, and they agreed to let me in to see Estelle. Sitting in the locked ward, I found a tense white woman in her early thirties. I told her that John had asked me to come, and when she heard this, she threw her arms around me. I had been blessed by John. I had come to save her.

I had no idea why Estelle was there and wasn't at all sure it was a good idea to get her out. We chatted and made friends, but after the effusive greeting, she was guarded with me. She was evasive about why she was there. There was no reason, she said. She had just been picked up by the cops and brought here.

When she gave me permission to talk to a nurse, I learned more. It seemed Estelle had been using drugs and had had a kind of psychotic reaction out on the street, which had drawn a crowd. With Estelle sedated and now calm, they were still evaluating what to do. After several more visits, they let me take Estelle out, after I had signed agreeing to act as her guardian.

Estelle's family more or less accidentally became my first Family Center clients. It was from her and her family that I learned enough to begin the work I wanted to do. After Estelle had been released from the hospital, I started visiting her and her five children in their home in a housing development more or less weekly, though sometimes I would meet with Estelle alone. Her story was one of perpetual fear and hardship—heartbreaking, but not uncommon among her neighbors.

Estelle grew up in foster homes. Like Charmaine, in almost every home she stayed in, Estelle had been molested by one of the family's males. In addition to this, the foster mothers had used her as a Cinderella, making her clean up after the other children and do the housekeeping. She was never safe. She was never in control of her life; she never felt loved. As she grew up, her feistiness helped create a hard shell, covering the softer feelings she was harboring but could not let out—not even to herself. As an adult and as a mother, she was tough. She acted as if she could take care of everything. She yelled a lot at her children—and at anyone else who got in her way.

We would all sit on her living room floor and talk. There would be complaints, and a sense that no one could possibly measure up to her expectations. The house was usually in shambles, though with five children it was hard to think how else it might have been, and Estelle worked hard to keep at least some kind of order. Even as we talked, she would get up to do laundry, making sure that her children had clean and pressed clothes every day for school.

In one way this behavior was an act of pride, making sure, in Estelle's words, that her kids didn't look like "dirty kids from the projects." But there was also more to it. While all the yelling and criticism seemed to denote anger and disappointment toward her children, washing and ironing their clothes was a way that she showed her love and her pride in them. The five kids had three different fathers, and had very distinctive temperaments. Two of the girls were feisty, like their mom, while the third was sweet and meek, always helping her siblings and her mother. One boy was tough, a street fighter, and the other boy was interested in books and learning. Sitting on the floor with Estelle and the children, we would talk about what was going on between them, who was doing what to whom, and what someone else thought this meant. The children were uncannily perceptive and enjoyed analyzing themselves this way. It was almost a kind of game. We identified actions that were unhealthy, and qualities and relationships that were extraordinarily strong. There was a strong capacity for joy in Estelle's family, happy moments that ran alongside the constant stress and anger.

What I learned from these sessions was what I was also learning from David Kantor, and from my readings of Salvador Minuchin, the godfather of family therapy. As family therapists, we could track what roles different family members played, what the "family game" or "family structure" was, and what the predictable family patterns were, pretty much all on a behavioral level—who was close to whom, who was distant, who wielded overt power, who wielded covert power, who was the family scapegoat, and who was being protected. As I recall, no one in Estelle's family ever cried. The "soft" emotions remained hidden.

I realized that in order to go deeper into what was making this family's life so chaotic and difficult (and it was chaotic, sometimes in scary ways), I needed to get to know Estelle better, and she needed to let down some of her guard and find the hurt and fear beneath her rage. She described her life to me as that of a quasi-junkie. She would put her kids on the school bus every day and then get together with friends to get high. Most of the day revolved around drugs. This was a community where people supported each other through a film of smoke, where their pain was muted, making life possible, but at a cost. It became clear to me that this group was a lifeline for its members. All of the women in it depended on a welfare check. Some, like Estelle, worked part time for a modest salary, but most of them were unemployed.

As months passed, Estelle freed herself from the destructive pattern of drug use. Though she had only been smoking weed, it was nonetheless an addiction, and as she moved away from marijuana she felt better physically and began to see her life more clearly. But with this change she also found herself isolated, having lost her mooring with the morning drug group, which she no longer attended. For me, these experiences produced a profound insight—my first major lesson in this new venture. Naturally formed support groups, albeit in this case organized around drug use, were an effective antidote to the isolation that so often comes from being poor, living in dangerous situations, having histories of fearful encounters, and more often than not simply feeling overwhelmed.

Estelle had gotten clean, but losing her support group was a hard price to pay. I felt responsible. By now the development of The Family Center was getting underway, but I was also still holding onto my private practice, where I ran a therapy group. Estelle had just taught me that if I was going to encourage a client to change her behavior, I also needed to help her replace her support group. In a desperate and perhaps foolhardy effort, I suggested she join my women's group.

I was not at all sure what the outcome of this action would be. The women in the group were all college-educated or beyond, from a reasonably homogenous upper-middle-class background, savvy with therapy jargon, and relatively comfortable with each other. Estelle, on the other hand, came from a very different background—how would they all respond to one another? But I took the chance. I got permission from the group to bring in a new member. I explained what the group was about to Estelle. And she came.

At the first meeting with Estelle, the group, using a gestalt model, sat on pillows arranged in a circle on the floor. Estelle and I sat on pillows in the center of the circle. I asked her to go around to each person in the circle and to tell them one thing about herself, and to ask the other woman something about herself. Then

I asked that each of them say something they noticed about each other. My heart was in my mouth. I felt desperately protective of Estelle—until the first exchange. When she began the conversation with her first counterpart, they began opening up to each other in a way I had never heard before in these group meetings. The floodgates parted, and each encounter seemed richer than the last. Estelle was in! And here was my second lesson. My first had been the importance of a group to support its members. Now I had also learned that mixing the types of people in the group might enrich everyone's experiences and their ability to open up.

Several months after this breakthrough therapy session, The Family Center program was ready to be launched in two housing projects, and it was not long afterward that I walked into Colleen's apartment for the first time.

After we had been operating for a few months, it occurred to me that Estelle could be an invaluable asset to our small staff. She was smart, she was drug-free, and in the time that we had known one another, she had achieved a good measure of control over herself and her life. She knew about troubled families from the inside. If she started working for us, it would give her a purpose, and The Family Center would benefit immensely. So, I offered her a job, and she took it.

3

THEORY AND PRACTICE

Thinkers/Doers

PARENTING JOURNEY HAS DRAWN FROM MANY SOURCES IN developing our theory and practices over the years. Of these influences, the contributions of David Kantor and Salvador Minuchin stand out as particularly significant.

David Kantor's theory, structural-analytic psychotherapy, was part of the very earliest development of The Family Center, before we had an organization or even a name. Elements of his theory, such as critical identity image, boundary profile, four player parts, and family typology, were especially instrumental as we developed our own therapeutic exercises and programs. The terms he invented, though, were not easily accessible, and my job in part was often to explain them.

Kantor's concept of critical identity image is similar to more traditional psychoanalytic thinking in terms of eliciting past experience that is directly tied to present behavior. Unlike traditional psychotherapy, though, critical identity image doesn't require long explorations of family history in order to determine the origins of troubled behavior. Instead, the therapist seeks the "critical" or salient past event that may be triggered by a heated subject in the present moment. Kantor's concept includes finding positive images as well as negative ones, allowing people to discover past experiences that have given them the strength they need to deal with present hardships.

Critical identity image has played a significant role in our therapeutic approach with clients. Take, for example, the story of Sheila and Peter.

Sheila and Peter were having terrible fights that didn't seem to make sense. One such fight occurred over the painting of the back door of their house. The couple had agreed on all the colors, and the painter was about to arrive. Sheila went off to work, and Peter stayed home to oversee the painting. As Peter and the painter were looking at the paints, Peter decided to change the color of the back door. When Sheila arrived home, she immediately noticed that the door was a different color than the one she and Peter had agreed upon, and she became very angry. Peter was confused by the strength of her anger, which he felt didn't match the situation, especially since Sheila said that she didn't mind the color he had chosen.

Their therapist looked for the structure of the event that had triggered the outburst—a "critical image"—something that reminded Sheila of a very terrifying experience somewhere in her past. The therapist abstracted the content of the story Sheila and Peter had told him, and repeated it back to them.

"Sheila, you left your house this morning, knowing that something would happen which you had both agreed upon. When you returned, you found that your expectation had not been fulfilled and that something else had happened instead. Tell me, when in your life did this happen before?"

Sheila welled up with tears and began sobbing, then she told them the following story.

She was 5 years old, a Jewish girl living in France during the war. Her parents took her into the countryside to visit a pretty church. They got to the gate of the church and were happily greeted by three nuns. There were lots of wooden shoes in the hallway, which intrigued Sheila, but none fit her, so one of the nuns asked if Sheila wanted to go with her to find a pair that would fit. Sheila eagerly agreed. When she returned along the long hallway to the place where she had left her parents, they were not there. She ran to the doorway and saw them walking away down the road. She yelled and screamed, but they did not turn back. Sheila did not see them again for 3 years. They had taken her to a nunnery for protection against the Nazis, who were invading the countryside where they lived.

Peter and Sheila were engulfed in tears at the end of Sheila's story. Having heard this memory, everyone could see that the structure of the two stories was the same, and given this new perspective, the content of the current one no longer mattered. The color of the door no longer mattered. They now knew that when Sheila was faced with an unexpected change, she might take a deep dive into the painful past, leaving other people wondering what was going on.

Helping Sheila to identify this event in her past enabled the therapist to make the crucial connection between a past event and current behavior, between past trauma and present dysfunction. He was helping Sheila and Peter uncover the connection between what had happened in Sheila's childhood that was exerting an unseen control over her present relationships.

While critical identity image has been instrumental as a way of helping clients gain insight into their problems, boundary profile relates directly to the dynamics between therapist and client. Kantor's theory here expresses the often hidden or disregarded fact that in a therapeutic relationship, the therapist and the client each bring a personal history to the relationship that dictates how they hear and see situations and problems—and each other.

Kantor emphasized the critical necessity for therapists to be aware of these unconscious biases that direct how we understand and focus on events, and increase the likelihood that we may disagree on how we see a situation. How and where we choose to look affects what we see. These biases can come from our expertise and training, our values, and especially our own personal experiences. When people work in human services or a mental health clinic, for example, they are likely to look for internal deficits that have pathological connotations and tend to emphasize what is wrong or missing in an individual. If they work with a family systems orientation, they are likely to look at what seems amiss in the family patterns. When people work in the social justice arena, they are likely to look outside at biases, racism, economic issues—what is missing, inhibiting, and/or provocative in the community environment. They may tend to see more assets in the individual than the mental health worker does. Each of these approaches and their various permutations can be helpful, but each, especially when adhered to uniquely, can and does create blind spots.

Personal characteristics and histories unconsciously influence our reactions not only in a therapy situation but in our lives outside of therapy as well. Imagine a white police officer pulling over two men of the same age who are driving similar cars, for the same traffic violation—say a broken taillight. Even if the police officer's motivation and behavior appear identical in both cases, if one driver is black, and the other white, each is likely to experience the interaction differently. The black man might experience the encounter with fear and resentment, while the white man is more likely to feel annoyed but physically safe. Likewise, it is quite possible the police officer will not react exactly the same way toward the black man and the white man, coming from his own personal experience and biases.

This kind of self-knowledge and sensitivity to differences and different experiences is an essential part of our training. So too has been Kantor's notion of four player parts. Kantor identified four primary roles an individual might play in a family situation. He named these roles mover, follower, opposer, and bystander. These, he said, were the universal roles members of a group bring to any group interaction. Well-developed individuals, he observed, can use all four roles depending on circumstances, even though they will inevitably have a preference for one role over another.

Families, for example, develop patterns of how they function depending on how these roles align within the group. A smoothly functioning family will exhibit a dominant pattern, but is capable of realigning in the face of new or challenging circumstances. A complicated organism like a family usually needs a mover to lead, followers to accept the leadership, an opposer or two to challenge assumptions, and a bystander to observe from a distance and

understand. And these roles may well shift around to accommodate varying situations. On the other hand, a family where one
or more individuals are frozen in a single role—as "opposers"
for example, who always disagree and are ready to fight—will
likely find itself dysfunctional. A family with no mover will find
it difficult to move.

Kantor's emphasis on the family as an interrelated organism
focuses the attention of the therapist on individuals in their relationships rather than on individuals as self-contained entities
with distinct sets of problems. In this way, the four player parts
direct the therapist's attention to the family dynamic in order to
understand the behavior of the individual.

The fourth key element of Kantor's theory is family typology.
This posits that there are three basic family structures: closed,
open, and random. Closed families are hierarchical, with a single
decision maker, who is often the father. Open families are more
democratic, and decisions are more likely to be shared and different voices heard. In random families, there are few boundaries,
and members tend to do what they each feel like doing. Each
of these structures, in Kantor's view, can be either successful or
unsuccessful. He perceived, though, that therapists tend to have
open-structure systems in their own families, while clients often
have closed or hierarchical families. A common error therapists
make, he says, is to assume that the well-functioning family is one
that is structured like their own.

These distinct family types are heavily influenced by culture and values, and attempting to change values—for example from a top-down autocratic system to a more democratic
decision-making structure—can be ineffective, and potentially
frustrating and insulting to the client family. In Kantor's theory,

the goal of therapy is to help families achieve success within their particular structure, not to attempt to change that structure in favor of the therapist's conception of which may be more positive.

If one were to apply the lens of family typology to Parenting Journey, our organization and use of space might qualify as a random structure; Kantor's obsession with creating evaluation forms that made sense would be a closed structure; and the way most of us related to clients and to each other would be open.

After David Kantor left us in the mid-90s, we were lucky enough shortly thereafter to work with one of the fathers of family therapy, Dr. Salvador Minuchin. Being exposed to Minuchin's work as a student had contributed significantly to my understanding of family therapy practices, and now we had the honor of working with him in person. Then in his retirement, Sal Minuchin volunteered with us one a day a week for 10 years, helping to train and supervise our staff while at the same time making major contributions to Parenting Journey's theoretical underpinnings. His structural family therapy was a keystone for us, as it has been for many others.

Minuchin began his career as a psychoanalyst, but while working with delinquent boys in a New York reform school, he quickly realized that without knowing the boys' parents and families, he could make little or no progress. He decided to bring families into the institution and began, in the mid-1960s, what many recognize as the first family therapy experiment. Although a trained Freudian, Minuchin focused on what was going on between people rather than solely on an individual's intrapsychic process. His premise was that a child's problems had to be seen in the context of the family.

In simplest terms, Minuchin's structural family therapy approach means looking at family interactions and behavioral patterns in order to identify and treat pathologies that affect its members. One child might be the "identified patient," but Minuchin focused on the whole family, looking for patterns, roles, power dynamics, who was close to whom, who was distant, who was the scapegoat, who made the decisions. His orientation in that regard was similar to David Kantor's.

Minuchin showed us that every family has a "dance"—roles and rituals they follow, knowingly or not—and that if we understand the family dance, we can help them change destructive steps for healthier ones. He enhanced our ability to understand visible symptoms from a wider angle, and to see that the individual in a family who is manifesting the symptoms is not often the true patient. When Billy climbed up on the roof of his school, he initially appeared to be the person in his family most in need of help. But through meeting with Billy's entire family, we were able to discover that it was actually Billy's mother and sister who were the troubled members, and Billy was one of the strongest members, willing to show what was going on. It was the family environment that had brought on the initial symptoms that Billy was displaying. It was the family that could be destructive, and the family that could help.

In his work with families, Minuchin was both supportive and confrontational. He could be effusive with congratulations, and also bluntly critical of how family members behaved with one another. He wasn't afraid of shaking up the family and pointing out obvious problems in relationships. He believed that helping families see negative patterns and relationships could point parents, spouses, and siblings toward reshaping their usual way of interacting. He also had an infectious optimism that communicated itself to clients and was therapeutic in its own right.

Once he got a sense of who was who and where everyone stood in a family, Minuchin could help people see—sometimes literally, by moving them around in the room relative to each other—how they operated and where they were stuck. He often had families act out their problems, having them arrange themselves physically in patterns, asking a child, for example, to place himself among his family members according to where he felt his place was in the mother's affections. Or he would have an aggressive child stand back-to-back with a beaten-down, ineffectual mother and ask the mother how it was that she thought the child was bigger than she was.

A practice that was critical to Minuchin's way of working, and many other therapists as well, was something he called "joining" with families. "Joining" families meant developing rapport and closeness that put the family at ease and allowed them to trust him, which also helped them accept his sometimes stark assessments. Once trust was established, they could see that however confrontational he might be, Minuchin was "on their side" in their struggle to deal with their problems, and they would be honest and open with him.

While Minuchin and Kantor shared a focus on the family as the primary determinant of behavior, Minuchin was less explicitly theoretical in his practice. He was a dynamic therapist who worked mostly in the present moment, helping families notice their patterns—the ones that were effective and those that brought them difficulties. He would instruct family members to do things they felt uncomfortable doing; he often surprised them and caught them off guard. Visiting a girl locked in the inpatient unit of a mental hospital, he listened as the girl's mother, who had come with him, made demands on her daughter that were overwhelming and more than a little irrational. The mother's anxiety was taking up all the space. Finally, Minuchin asked the mother, "Tell me, why aren't YOU in the hospital?"

He believed that any family could find the internal strength to change their lives for the better. Like Kantor, Minuchin reminded us that when we are looking for deficits, it is critical that we also search for assets. Many trained professionals tend to look for what's missing; they don't probe or have the eye or instinct for seeking hidden strengths, resources, and possibilities. Minuchin was the great advocate for bringing this kind of understanding to bear. He saw beyond the surface, and his understanding of complexities was exceptional. He admired the strengths he saw, and he took those strengths as the keys to what would work. A typical question he would ask was, "So, tell me, how did you manage to get this far? What is your secret?" The question conveyed that he understood the severity of the struggle clients were going through, and that in spite of everything, they had found the wherewithal to get their family to seek help, which was as much to say that the clients had the strength to face up to and overcome their difficulties.

While David Kantor and Sal Minuchin helped develop Parenting Journey's fundamentals, other theoreticians and practitioners have also significantly influenced our work. John Bowlby was one of these. Beginning in the late 1950's, Bowlby's attachment theory determined that during the normal course of development, a child forms an intimate bond with the mother/caregiver, and the quality of that attachment profoundly influences the development of interpersonal behavior throughout the child's life. Disruptions or interference in that attachment have both short- and long-term negative effects on the child's emotional life, as well as on cognitive development. Bowlby also demonstrated that a child's attachment problems extend generationally. Poor or negative attachment impacts the child's own ability to bond when he or she becomes a parent.

Bowlby's work was expanded through his collaboration with Mary Ainsworth, who demonstrated the depth of an infant's and young child's emotional life. Ainsworth is also known for determining that the quality and level of secure or insecure attachment between child and caregiver affects outcomes at every subsequent developmental stage. More recent studies in brain development and the work of Daniel Siegel have further corroborated the effects on children who have experienced continuous stress due to insecure attachment, versus those children whose brains were allowed to develop without being under constant vigilance and fear. Donald Winnicott's object relations theory and developmental psychology have also contributed to our work.

When we started our organization, trauma was not nearly as well understood as it has come to be. Judith Herman, Bessel Van der Kolk, and others, have added to an overall increased understanding of trauma. Herman, a leading expert on post-traumatic stress and recovery, has written books and papers describing the power of traumatic shock, which can overwhelm the victim's usual sense of control, meaning, and connection with others, and can leave a person's ability to cope in shreds. She has increased our understanding of how disturbed levels of early attachment connect to trauma, and how long it can take and how complicated it can be to counteract the damage. Making sense of one's story, which is the object of many of our exercises, can be a stabilizing experience that can work to interrupt the common pattern of trauma repeating itself from parent to child.

Parenting Journey has also drawn upon ideas from our colleague Katya Fels Smyth, whose organization, The Full Frame Initiative, strives to "shift perspectives on poverty and violence to create well-being and justice." The Full Frame Approach to wellness—created by Smyth and Dr. Lisa Goodman—is an evidence-informed approach that takes into account the interplay between an individual's internal and external needs and what resources and relationships need to be brought into play in an ameliorative process. It is currently being used by several state agencies around the country. According to Smyth and Goodman, well-being requires assets in five domains of life: social connectedness, safety, stability, mastery, and meaningful access to relevant resources.

The Full Frame Approach, much like Kantor and Minuchin, also focuses on assets rather than deficits alone. Smyth's question is not "What is the matter with you?" but "What matters to you?" Shifting the therapeutic perspective from "What's *wrong* with you?" to "What's *right* with you?" supports clients' empowerment, orienting them toward an ability to take control of where it is that they want to go in the face of daunting circumstances.

From the beginning, our work at Parenting Journey has always centered on the strengths and resilience of our client families. Many of these families have lost, or given up, the capacity to imagine. But, as Rosamund Zander emphasizes in her two books, *The Art of Possibility* and *Pathways to Possibility,* one of the strengths we are all blessed with is creativity. If we can imagine realities for ourselves, she says, we will have the ability to work toward fulfilling them. Creativity, she reminds us, is an innate human capacity. It allows us to focus our energies on choices and change, on how our lives might be different from what they are. Our practices are designed with this in mind, to encourage the critical process of connecting the past with a reimagined future. In so doing we define ourselves rather than letting history alone define us.

As attachment theory has given us respect for the depth and pain of trauma experienced by so many of our client families, over the years we have also widened our lens to focus on the communities where they live. While our expertise is concentrated on the internal stress that external realities contribute to, we have become increasingly aware of the need to address not only the circumstances of individual parents' lives, but also the stresses that effect their entire communities. "When you are bombarded by poverty, uncertainty, and fear," says Alicia Lieberman, a leading expert on childhood trauma, "it takes a superhuman quality to provide the conditions for a secure attachment."

For us this has meant increasing our engagement with families' living circumstances and the civic actions required to make a difference in these areas. Even in our beginning years, The Family Center embraced the work of Saul Alinsky, the famous community activist of the 1950s and 1960s, in supporting and organizing campaigns focused around better housing, guaranteed minimum income for families on welfare, safety in the community, constant contact between teachers and parents in schools, and health fairs. This engagement remains a vital part of our organization today.

As important as all these theories and practitioners have been to Parenting Journey's development, it has still fallen to us to create practices that are useful to the people in our programs. In this, we have been lucky to have the masterful expertise of my dear friend and colleague Jody Scheier and other staff in developing techniques and programs, and teaching others of our staff how to think imaginatively with concrete interventions.

We have found that physical, active interventions are usually more effective than words. We have created exercises that challenge families, using psychodrama, family sculpture, role playing, gestalt exchanges, letter writing, drawings, and humorous games to get around defenses in order to access deep secrets and hurts, while maintaining emotional safety. This repertoire of evidence-based, strength-focused, experiential, and action-oriented therapies encourages the exploration of intrapsychic and interpersonal issues through enactment rather than simply talking. The interventions allow the body as well as the mind to come forward into the therapeutic milieu and tell the story. As Jacob Levi Moreno, the founder of psychodrama, put it, "The body remembers what the mind forgets."

Our programs at Parenting Journey have an overall coherence, but, as we have seen, they are built of many component parts: family therapy, social justice, psychoeducation, and family support, with each approach bolstering and informing the others. We don't regard our approach as a new theory of treatment. Instead, we see ourselves as continually evolving new interventions, building on and refining our original insights, and broadening our understanding of the elements that inhibit healthy family and community life and those that help make them strong.

4

VANTAGE POINTS

Maria is Angry, Sami is Frightened, Mom Keeps a Loaded Gun by the Door

MARIA

Maria was a quiet 12-year-old Latina girl who lived in a housing project with her mother, her mother's boyfriend, and two small siblings, aged two and four. She frequently didn't go to school, but when she did, she became what her teachers described as a "holy terror." She upended desks, screamed, and otherwise acted out angrily with both her peers and teachers. The principal complained to Maria's mother that she was unruly, and Maria was sent to a counselor for help. The diagnosis was anxiety disorder.

If, instead of being sent to a school counselor by herself, Maria had been visited at home by a family therapist or community worker, they would have found that Maria often did not go to school because she was staying home to help her mother take care of her two younger siblings. They would have found that Maria's mother, Angela, had crippling asthmatic attacks and painful arthritis, and that she sometimes left Maria alone to watch the younger kids while she visited a doctor or got some rest from her pain. Instead of the generalized diagnosis of "anxiety disorder," made from the limited vantage point of an office appointment, a family therapist who visited Maria at home might have been able to see that Maria was deathly afraid of something terrible happening to her mother, and of being left alone.

Maria's mother, Angela, had immigrated to the United States from Ecuador. At the age of 13, she suffered severe childhood trauma when she was abandoned by her parents in her hometown and left in the care of an aunt who died shortly thereafter. In a powerful act of mastery, bravery, and know-how, she managed to get herself to the United States border and into the country to rejoin her parents. Now, as an adult, residues of this childhood trauma were persisting. Angela still feared abandonment and self-medicated to be able to sleep and to be able to function.

At home, Maria was ordinarily a docile, polite child. It was only at school that she could let loose her rage, express her choked up feelings of fear, and feel in some ways free. It was also only in school that she could be seen as "symptomatic." Much as it was with Billy, for Maria, being seen as symptomatic was a rather ingenious way of calling attention to what actually needed attending to in her family.

As we can see in both Billy and Maria's stories, in many situations our current social work system doesn't easily allow for a broad crosscutting exploration of what is going wrong in a client's life. The common helping profession orientation is to separate problems into silos: addictions, teen pregnancy, domestic violence, homelessness, school failure, etc., and then to try to "fix" the problems that have been identified—such as diagnosing Maria with an anxiety disorder, or Billy with a bipolar disorder.

A mental health designation like this presumes a "disorder" or deviance from a norm, and it generally has a negative connotation. The "norm" that the *Diagnostic and Statistical Manual of Mental Disorders* (DSM) derives from has historically come from a cultural context of white, mostly male, privileged, usually educated, often medically trained professionals. There is no doubt about the usefulness of DSM diagnoses in many instances where differentiated diagnoses direct certain treatment plans. In many cases these treatments, whether chemical, talking therapy, and other types of therapeutic intervention, can save lives, alleviate stress, relieve depression, and prevent psychoses. However, there is a danger that DSM diagnoses may constitute blinders, and also that a mental health professional might be prone to diagnosing problems without being attuned to strengths.

Maria did show strengths. She showed maturity in being able to care for her siblings, almost like a second mother. She also cared for her mother, helping her manage the household. Other than in school, she behaved well so as not to rock the boat, either for herself or the rest of the family. To some, Maria's designation as the "parentified" child would be considered a problem, to others it would be a practical strength. Viewing Maria and her family through a systemic lens, a caregiver might want to rethink the original diagnosis and instead choose to see a contextually complex situation, rife with pain and bravery. Approaching the situation from this angle, one could try to find help at the family systems level by breaking up burdensome patterns in Maria's mother Angela's often physically painful life, and, at the community level, by finding resources and a social milieu which could provide comfort and support for Angela and her family. This approach would also recognize and appreciate Maria's creative skillfulness, albeit unconscious, in getting help for her family.

If a broad contextual approach, which includes a social justice orientation, replaces a medical, mental illness model, we may well adopt different interventions with predictably different consequences. Deeply exploring how the "we" interact with the "they" can radically change the nature of the relationship and the outcome of the encounter. This is especially relevant when the "we" are white "entitled" people with power and the "they" are people whose skin is black or brown and who may belong to very different cultures. This is hardly to say that all mental illness originates in a form of social injustice. However, we need to become sensitive to ways that a "we-they" mentality can subtly and unconsciously take hold and insert itself into a well-intended supportive and helping structure. Without such personal awareness and an openness to exploring the broader social and familial context, diagnosing (and/or incarcerating) a "deviant" may trump exploring the larger context, like altering neighborhood patterns of violence.

In all of this, there is a mental health language, a family systems language, and a context-sensitive, social justice language. Words matter. They denote emphasis, values, and locus of problem. Take for example the story of Silvia.

A 27-year-old Latina woman who had recently immigrated to the United States from Mexico, Silvia had a sick child and two other children to attend to, no family nearby, no reliable friends, and no place she knew of to go for help. She was terrified that

ICE (U.S. Immigration and Customs Enforcement) agents might separate her from her children, or send them all back to Mexico. She had a sporadic cleaning job, but was on the verge of homelessness. In spite of all of this, she managed to get her children to school every day, and even found the bus fare for one of her kids to go to a charter school outside of the neighborhood.

Caregivers and concerned friends variously told us that Silvia was: strong, stressed, isolated, anxious, brave, unstable, powerless, powerful, depressed, hopeless, and possibly psychotic. Some of these words apply to traditional psychological diagnoses. Some apply more to a social and cultural context. Some are positive and acknowledge Silvia's fortitude, while others carry negative judgments.

Depending on where a helping professional focuses on this list, he or she will prioritize an approach relevant to that perception of the problem. We have to keep in mind that when we judge someone like this and apply a label, we are using our own experience to evaluate another's. When life experiences differ significantly, a caregiver might well light on a negatively connoted label/diagnosis. What is unfamiliar can seem deviant, unhealthy, and fearful. If there are conflicting opinions, and if they are exacerbated by a power differential, applying labels is frequently an easier way out than becoming curious and opening up candid, "difficult" conversations. The label takes the place of self-introspection, as well as curiosity about the other. When this thinking occurs among service providers and their clients, we see risks in misinterpretation and often unintended consequences.

A woman who fears that her abusive ex-husband will show up and kill her and her children, even if she has a restraining order, might keep a loaded gun in a closet near the front door. To the mother, that loaded gun is her biggest family asset. To the child welfare worker, that gun is the biggest threat to the family's safety. When looking at the broader frame, the worker takes account of the mother's position, and respects her understanding that the police may well be too slow to respond if the ex-husband shows up. The discussion then becomes, "What can we do to make sure you and your children are safe, both from your ex-husband and from the loaded gun?" This discussion, which takes in the nuances of the situation and respects both parties involved, may have a more positive outcome for everyone than if the child welfare worker simply demands that the mother get rid of the gun.

As a service provider, listening carefully to a person's whole story, respecting his or her concerns, and looking at the widest, most complete picture we can, helps us work together with the client family to find the solution that makes the most sense for *that* family.

SAMI

Sami was 15 years old, the son of a Pakistani family. A handsome boy, he had been a good athlete and popular with kids in his neighborhood. But then his father lost his job and the family had to move. Soon afterward Sami became depressed. He started refusing to go to school and no longer played sports or wanted to have friends around. He stayed in his bed a lot, often hearing his parents fighting with each other.

The family's new apartment was located across from a notorious public housing project. Huddles of young men stood around on the street at all hours. Cars frequently drove up and stopped, and deals were made through the windows. Every weekend large white limousines parked on the street, and it was general knowledge that men came up from the city to do business. In addition to a flourishing drug culture, the local school was one of the lowest performing in the city, and both teachers and students showed a kind of apathy that Sami had never seen before. He wanted to learn, but it seemed as though nobody wanted to teach him. He had shared this dismaying information with his parents, but perhaps because of their own troubles, they hadn't seemed to focus on what he had been saying.

Every day, it felt harder for him to get up, to go to school, and to concentrate. The classrooms were disorganized, and the teachers merely focused on trying to maintain discipline. Sami noticed that some of his classmates were hanging out with kids he knew to be dealing drugs. This frightened him. After school, he would carefully pick his way home and return immediately to his room. He started not showing up for meals, telling his parents he had no appetite.

Just as with the other families we have looked at, there are many ways to understand Sami's story, all of which might have truth to them. If one looks at these symptoms from a family systems perspective, one might hypothesize that the family member carrying the symptoms is the son, while the real struggle lies in the parental relationship. Sami might be "detouring" the family issues—attracting attention and energy to himself in order to keep a family crisis at bay. Although he might be the symptom bearer, the one crying for help, like Billy and Maria, he might not be the one who needed it most. Neither he nor his parents would likely be conscious that this was what was going on.

If one looks at this same set of symptoms from a community perspective, one might focus on different information and make an alternative interpretation. One might find that the school is poor, boring to a good student, and the neighborhood a scary place to be, driving Sami to stay at home. A possible solution might take the form of galvanizing support for community meetings to address the dangerous aspects of the neighborhood and to tackle the low caliber of teaching and apathetic administration that is dragging students as well as teachers down.

These are huge issues, requiring time, effort, community support, and connections to its institutions and leadership, but a determined effort might make a difference to Sami and to many more.

It's also possible that Sami was not doing homework and not going to school regularly because he couldn't read well, and was embarrassed, even though nobody had noticed. In his former school he had gotten additional tutoring help in reading. One might also find that one of the reasons Sami couldn't read well was that he had a hard time seeing and needed glasses—something no one had considered, not even himself.

As we noted in chapter three, in order to experience a sense of well-being, one must have at least some assets in each of the five "domains" of wellness—social connectedness, safety, stability, mastery, and meaningful access to relevant resources—developed by Katya Fels Smyth and The Full Frame Initiative. In Sami's case, his depression may very well have been connected to the lack of adequate feelings of satisfaction in each of these areas of his life.

Looking more closely at these domains, the first, social connectedness, comes from the perception that each of us, regardless of who we are and where we come from, need relationships where we are needed and can depend on others, and groups where we feel we belong. For Sami, a sudden move to a new neighborhood and school disrupted his ability to have satisfying contact with both his peers and his family. The second domain, safety, includes the ability to express core parts of our identity without danger or shame, and in Sami's case was also directly reflected in the lack of physical safety he felt in his new neighborhood. The third domain, stability, or having a sense of predictability and familiarity on a daily or weekly level and the sense that small disturbances won't set off cascades of destructive events, was also upset by the family's move and Sami's parents' relationship; as was the fourth domain, mastery, the sense that we can take control of and affect our environment, relationships, and future. The fifth domain, meaningful access to relevant resources, pertains to living in a community that meets core needs such as good education, health facilities, and neighborhood safety was also not a reality for Sami. At that moment in his life, Sami was suffering from a deficit in all five of these areas.

While each of us shares a common striving for assets in these five domains, we all experience these areas in different and deeply personal ways. Most of our behavior is intended to move us ahead in one or another of these domains in ways that don't create significant trade-offs in other areas.

For example, waking up an hour earlier to get to a new job farther from home may not be much of a trade-off. But if it means coming home later and missing visiting hours at a parent's nursing home, it does. Sometimes we can find a way to minimize the trade-off so that what wasn't worth it before, now is: for example, convincing the nursing home to make an exception, allowing visiting after hours twice a week. Being able both to decide *for ourselves* what's "worth it," and to navigate life in ways that builds our assets in as many areas as possible and minimizes trade-offs, fosters our overall well-being.

We experience positive change when the trade-offs are, indeed, worth it. But how each of us weighs trade-offs is uniquely personal. Is it worth it to take a different shift that pays more? For some, the answer might be yes. But for a mother who has lost a son to gun violence, and who is intent on being home in the evenings with her other son, the answer might be no.

As it was for Sami, when one or more of these asset areas were at a low level, or close to empty, well-being deteriorates and goes missing. It's then that the signs of distress we call "symptoms" appear. They are not necessarily mental health–related, although a severe deficit in any one (or more) of the asset areas could probably lead to a DSM diagnosis, as may have been the case with Sami's depression. On the other hand, one could also attribute the "symptoms" to a family dysfunction, or to a community overcome by the reinforcing effects of poor schools, poor health, drug dealing, violence, and the like—all commonly fueled by pervasive racism and poverty.

To successfully help affect the lives of families living in deprived conditions like Sami and Maria—both externally and internally—an approach that combines innovative mental health and family system approaches with social justice awareness and action may well be the most promising. By widening our lens, merging social justice and mental health orientations, and understanding their interconnectedness we possess a stronger arsenal to approach complex problems. This requires a no-holds-barred commitment to erasing inequities wherever possible, and supporting rather than blaming persons overwhelmed with challenges and inadequate resources. It also requires a self-empowering frame of mind on the part of both the family members and the helpers—a sense that "despite the difficulties here, I can do this."

To achieve a self-empowering frame of mind, individuals need to have experiences in which they have control, choices, and the skills to achieve what they are choosing to do. They need to have areas of mastery in their lives. They have to recognize their strengths and capacities, their moments of success, and they have to be recognized for them. Going even further, they may need to free themselves from the demons of past trauma—whether it be fear of abandonment, sexual or physical assault, the anguish of neglect, or the experience of violence done to one's own self or witnessing it perpetrated on another. They have to deal with the suppressed experiences that are holding them back from mastery over life.

Recognizing and facing these suppressed traumas, and feeling cared about, can lead to changing relational and other behaviors. To grow, individuals need to be treated with respect, especially as they are likely to have experienced the burning sensations of stigma and shame. Positive changes in family relationships will have a marked effect on an individual's sense of well-being and of their own empowerment. To do this, people need to make sense of what has happened to them, and they need to find their voices in order to speak about their experiences. They have to know that their experiences matter, to themselves and to others.

5

PIVOTAL INTERVENTIONS

Playing, Experimenting, and Creating

As the Family Center developed, we created a series of interventions that were intriguingly effective. I should say, before describing successes, that there were mistakes made, chaotic events, events with low attendance, and particular difficulty in attracting men, even though we had male staff and groups for boys. There were stumbles, crises, and disappointing outcomes. A very committed staff, largely made up of relatively untrained people (some with GEDs, others with some counseling experience, and some with formal clinical training), explored and carried out the vision we had in our minds of a rather simple series of interventions, learning as we went from our clients.

Some people burned out along the way, and some felt they were tasked with too many different things, making their lives chaotic and unmanageable. I was the team leader, and it took time for me to learn that not everybody can do everything just because it needs doing. We did eventually compartmentalize a bit, but we never got to the point where staff said "that's not my job" when something needed to be done. Everyone who came to work with us understood that it would be a big challenge. Many of our staff came from communities similar to the ones we were working in, and had escaped relatively unscathed, where some of their family members had not. These staff members expressed a desire to "give back" to the community, and give back they did!

One of our essential goals was to create a therapeutic program in a low-income community which would not be bound by federal and state reimbursement categories of "treatment." In order to accomplish this, for ourselves and for others for whom this might become a model, it needed to be cost efficient. This meant we could not, and actually did not want, to hire a mostly well-trained professional staff. We could not, because we could not afford them, and we did not want to because when we tried hiring more traditionally trained mental health workers, they consistently resisted our "looser" boundaries and experimental approaches to working with clients.

To make our program a viable model, it had to be relatively cheap, and it had to be creative. In this effort, three interventions stand out as examples. One was a mother and daughter group, the second a community soap opera, and the third a pregnancy prevention program. We later built elements of these three interventions into Parenting Journey's programs and curricula.

MOTHERS AND DAUGHTERS

Nadia was one of our early staff members at The Family Center. An elegant young black woman originally from Trinidad, she had lived in England before moving to the United States. She was chic and had a strong sense of style that was immediately noticed by the women and girls she worked with. As weeks went by, we noticed more girls, and even some mothers, sporting white-beaded necklaces over conservative sweaters and blouses, resembling the style that Nadia wore. Mini Nadias began appearing all over the neighborhood.

Nadia's passion was helping mothers and daughters relate better and more comfortably with each other. We developed a plan to have a group of mothers and daughters meet together, as well as separately, to discuss sensitive subjects like menstruation, the biology of sex, safe sex, and pregnancy prevention. After an initial meeting with the mothers, and then one with the daughters, we had them all come together to watch the first part of a movie called *On Becoming a Woman*. The movie, which had been created by a similar group of mothers and daughters in Atlanta, depicted women discussing these uncomfortable topics, and helped our group feel freer in their discussions. The plan seemed to be going well. However, the next part of the process turned out to be much more difficult than Nadia had expected.

She made an appointment to meet first with the mothers, asking them to bring an object that reminded them of their younger teenaged selves, something that might help them get back to the feelings they had had at the age when their bodies began changing. She hoped that this exercise would help them connect better with their daughters. But when she met with the mothers to discuss what they would tell their daughters, Nadia discovered that many of them felt ignorant about what menstruation actually was, why it happens, and what the female anatomy and reproductive system looked like. They told Nadia that no one had ever explained these things to them, and they were fearful of being challenged for answers by their daughters.

The mothers felt angry. Pent-up feelings of anger toward their own parents for not educating them surfaced as they remembered the fear and confusion they had experienced with their first periods. Now they were projecting this fear and anger onto their own daughters. Some didn't see the need to tell their daughters anything. Some saw the very onset of their daughters' menses as a threatening indication that their child was growing up, and might soon be leaving home. There were a lot of patterns of what we call enmeshment and insecure attachment present in the group. They started to panic.

But it wasn't just the women in the group who were feeling this way. Nadia found that she herself was feeling fearful about her own personal memories that she was bringing to this exercise. She suggested that the women write letters to their mothers, even if they were now dead, saying what they were feeling in reliving this experience of having been "abandoned" at that scary point in their lives.

While the mothers were writing letters, Nadia met with the girls and asked them what their mothers had told them about these sensitive topics. The answers were all the same: "nothing." Then Nadia asked them to come up with questions they might have for their mothers relating to menstruation, sex, pregnancy, and female biology. Her plan was for the girls to ask their mothers these questions. But she realized that these conversations would have to be delayed until she could help get the mothers adequately educated and prepared.

When the mothers and daughters reconvened after a period of coaching for the mothers, and assurances by Nadia that she would help them if they did not have answers, the group got together over a dinner.

Then the unexpected happened. After a very few minutes, one of the girls, speaking to another in a low voice, told her friend that she had been sexually molested by her mother's boyfriend. One of the mothers overheard the conversation, and in a sympathetic gesture told the girl she was not alone. This ignited a conversation that had not been planned. When the other mothers heard what the sympathetic mother had said, *all* of them joined in to confess that they too had at some point been molested. They spoke, and the girls listened intently. None of them interrupted the flow of their mothers' talk. Charmaine, who was one of the members of the group along with her daughter Mia, said, with tears flowing down her face, "Sometimes I think because of what happened to me when I was younger I can't ever have a good relationship with a man."

None of us had anticipated so intimate an encounter so early in the group meetings, and its explosive nature both bonded and scared the participants. The girls embraced each other, the mothers hugged one another, and then they all hugged with tears and the recognition that something very important had just happened. While relief might not be the right word to describe what the mothers and daughters were feeling, it certainly entered into the play of emotions.

Nadia described her own response in her notes to her supervisor: "At this point I felt very lost, depressed, mad, sad, and helpless. I just didn't want to hear anymore. I looked at the mothers and said to myself, 'I don't want to hear this. I can't help you. I don't know how to help you, to make it easy for all of you. Plus, I don't know what I can do to help you when I don't feel I can even help myself.' And then I looked at the girls and I felt I wanted to do something for them, anything so they won't reach my age and feel the way I am feeling right now."

Her statement reflected not only her empathy but also the reemergence of memories of the sexual abuse Nadia herself had suffered, and her sense of helplessness toward being able to effectively help the others since she was so triggered herself. It also defined her commitment to finding a better way out for the next generation. In other notes to her supervisor, she wrote, "I want things to work out right—this is an obsession." And it *was* her obsession. She became totally committed to finding another way forward.

Nadia redirected her curriculum in response to these unexpected sexual disclosures. Part of doing this, she realized, was that she had to take into account how her own personal experience of abuse had affected her response in the moment. In a bold move, she decided to acknowledge to the group in a subsequent meeting that she, too, had experienced sexual abuse.

This encounter with her own unfinished personal business and the way that she handled it initiated a deep exploration on the part of our team. As a group leader or therapist, was it appropriate to strategically expose one's own personal experiences? Could this tactic be put to good use? And if so, when, how, and to what end? All the rules of therapy cautioned against self-disclosure to clients. But we could see the value, even in Nadia's partial disclosure, of sharing something so personal and painful. Her instincts told her that doing so would bring her into the circle, which was where she wanted to be.

Sorting this out after the fact, we realized that group leaders and family therapists could make greater contributions working with clients as partners rather than on different sides of an imaginary hierarchical divide—as long as the leader had worked out a way of living with her pain and would not become disabled in talking about it. To the extent that she was more knowledgeable, had worked through what her own past trauma meant to her, and had experienced the relief of being able to share it with others, she could lead the way through the painful thicket and model to the others that there was a way to move forward.

Nadia spent time working these issues through with her supervisor, reducing her isolation, and sharing her secret, until she felt ready to move on and use this revelation as part of her tool kit. This episode was a turning point in our development as an organization. Since then, facilitators' selective sharing of aspects of their own lives has become central to the Parenting Journey model.

The women in Nadia's group agreed to meet separately for a period of time, mothers in one group, and daughters in the other. We were entering areas that were new to all of us. This instance of an overheard conversation had opened up the most emotionally charged area possible. It was "unintended" at the time, but it opened up what was inhibiting many of the women and girls in this group, and it led the way to concrete conversations aimed at preventing further abuse among their families. Nadia's focused processing of her own issues provided the opportunity to lead the group back to a safer place, one where they could problem-solve rather than only relive their pain.

The two groups began working on plans and goals to prevent further abuse, instead of the original plan of pursuing sex education and pregnancy prevention. Both the mothers' group and the daughters' group came up with goals that were virtually identical and reflected a growing sense of empowerment. When the two groups came together, they distilled their ideas into eight goals.

1. They agreed to talk about sexual abuse issues with each other and to support one another.
2. They agreed that having been assaulted was not their fault and promised to support each other when they slipped into feeling it was.
3. They agreed to tell someone in the group if it happened again, knowing that that person would be committed to doing something about it.
4. They agreed to confront the offenders—with help from the group if necessary—and anyone else who stood by and did not help them.
5. They agreed to work on enhancing their self-esteem.
6. They engaged in conversations about what love is as opposed to being hurt and taken advantage of.
7. They agreed to take actions: have someone talk to them about sexual and violent abuse, get the police to protect them, get help with their problems from the local hospital, call the housing authority, and call the governor.

8. They wanted to visit the crisis team at the local hospital, the courthouse, and local clinics.

While not all of these agreements were realized, the acts of coming up with the ideas and having the conversations were themselves empowering. The girls were all quite dogmatic about making sure everyone was on board with this plan, and they assigned concrete assignments to each other—who would do what, when they would do it, and how they would do it. The girls wanted to write a book on the subject and to perform a play. They each created a play (not necessarily about being abused, as not all of them had been), videotaped it, and then showed it to their mothers. The other girls in the group took the roles needed for each other's dramas. The subjects were similar—their own abuse or the abuse they witnessed in their families, often against their mothers. These were painful stories, but once the girls' secrets were out and they realized the relief they felt sharing these deep experiences with others, their enthusiasm galloped along, and they actually had fun creating some real and mythical scenes.

Meanwhile, the mothers were meeting with Nadia, and mostly focusing back on the original plan—to pay attention to how they wanted to tell their daughters about menstruation, sex, and protection. Nadia gave the mothers research assignments to find out from the local library things they wanted to know about the human body—menstruation, sex, pregnancy, and how they happen. The mothers then came together with their children, armed with their new knowledge, and tried to answer their daughters' questions. When they could not, it became an opportunity for mothers and daughters to go to the library together to research such things as fallopian tubes, ovaries, ovulation, the menstrual cycle, and eventually, birth control. It was clear that both the mothers and the daughters loved these learning expeditions and the discovery of the library. The mothers also commented that along with this knowledge came a new comfortableness with their daughters.

After about a year, the mothers resumed their conversations with Nadia about their personal experiences with abuse, which were also sometimes stories about incest. This group was so rich with ways of capturing the attention of the other members, provoking intellectual interest, and illuminating the emotional realities of mothers and daughters, that it gave rise to a two-generational Parenting Journey approach that we had hardly thought possible. The mothers and daughters in the group were becoming friends.

What, specifically, did we take from these lessons? We learned that family members can become close if the environment is safe. Safety was assured by the group leader, and especially by the nature of the group itself. We learned that being able to share a grim truth relieves the pain to some extent, and that secrets are like clogged arteries, potentially dangerous and debilitating. We learned that selective personal sharing by the group leader lowered the assumption on the part of the clients that people like their group leader didn't experience the same kinds of traumas and stresses they themselves did. When Nadia felt the urge to share her experience, she was responding to the need of the group to feel more like peers—just women and girls opening up to each other. It relieved some of the feelings these women had that they were damaged goods. They could suddenly see themselves in Nadia, and this recognition further enhanced their own sense of "okayness," that they, too, were people who could manage despite their bad experiences and their pain.

We learned that there is an important place for educating oneself, for "doing something about" one's ignorance. Ignorance didn't need to be seen as just a fact of life. We learned that when people are motivated, they can do what they need to do to make their lives better. Many of these women were trapped in the belief that this was simply how life was. But no longer. They learned they had their own resources, and had or could get what they needed to help themselves. We learned that encouraging creativity and concrete visual representations were strong therapeutic tools. We learned that change really could and did happen.

Some interventions that originated in this group were carried over to Parenting Journey: writing letters to one's parents, bringing a special object to the group which might remind one of feelings from events past. Strategic self-disclosure changed the way we positioned ourselves. Drawing and acting out difficult experiences found their way into the curriculum as well.

One day, close to the end of the group, Nadia told the girls that, that day, they could do anything they wanted. Charmaine's daughter, Mia, said she wanted to visit a church she knew because the building was really beautiful. The group agreed to go to the church, and Mia was right; it was beautiful. Sitting inside, all the girls felt peaceful, and filled with the kind of awe a church is supposed to inspire. It was an extraordinary and fitting end to an extraordinary, though tumultuous, experience.

SOAP OPERA

One day, when I was sitting with Colleen on her couch, I was, as usual, being drowned out by the noise from two separate televisions, one in the living room, the other on a different channel in her bedroom. It wasn't that I couldn't hear; it was that I didn't know what to try to listen to—Colleen, the living room soap opera, or whatever was going on in the other room. She, on the other hand, seemed to juggle everything without difficulty. I marveled at this much noise making any kind of sense. Then I realized that maybe she wasn't actually listening to any of it, including her own nonstop voice. Maybe it was just the noise itself that she was hearing.

It occurred to me that, instead of looking at the television trials and tribulations of overprivileged people with whom Colleen had nothing in common, why not create something that would have meaning? Instead of TV soaps being background noise, why not make a soap that would actually grab her attention? In fact, why not make an active, living soap opera rather than spending time passively filling the void with senseless noise?

I mulled this idea over a bit, spoke to a few people about it, and some months later looked up my buddy Matt, a Harvard student who had run summer boys' groups in the housing developments. Matt was a theater major, fascinated by soap operas. I approached him with this idea and he was intrigued. He showed me copies of *Soap Opera Times*, which he collected. I described my idea a little more fully. In a different setting, I had witnessed the power of community-written and led theater, and knew the power it could have.

The concept was that he would take a video camera into a family's house—one of the families he knew from the boys' group. He'd suggest to the family members that they make a soap opera of life in the projects. From this one family, which turned out to be Charmaine's family, Matt would start the project, which would organically grow itself.

That was exactly what happened. As Matt started conversations with Charmaine's family and whoever else was in the apartment, they began spontaneously coming up with plots and subplots. A good thing about soap operas is that there are lots of different stories going on at the same time, sometimes with different characters, sometimes the same. This was perfect for an often-chaotic community, where bringing people together reliably was not in the cards.

The therapeutic underpinning of the soap opera was that this would be therapy by metaphor, claiming the creative and artistic talents of whoever volunteered to be part of what I began thinking of as the "Soap Troupe." As people gathered around Matt and his camera, they made up stories and identified the characters they needed for their plots. Then they went out to find people in the neighborhood who could help make their visions a reality. They were excited to do this; it caught their imaginations. More stories got added, and as stories were spun out, then improvised on camera, the participants had to figure out how to solve the narrative problems they had created.

My only rule for Matt was not to ask or otherwise identify anything that came up in the soap opera as something that was a real-life issue for any member of the cast. No "is this a problem in your life?" kinds of questions. The therapeutic effect would be done in metaphor by people raising issues that were familiar to them and then using their own ingenuity and creativity to solve them. No therapist needed. Matt would simply guide the process, call the meetings, video the sequences, and help people see their options as to where to take the story to the next step. Sometimes there was a large cast of about 20, sometimes just a dialogue between two people.

One simple vignette occurred between two teenage girls on the phone. Nakeisha was lacing into her friend Donna about doing drugs in the hallway. Donna was angry at Nakeisha for butting into her affairs, and told her to mind her business and that she had too much on her mind to deal with this right now. A short scene like this, acted with great feeling, led Matt to ask them where they wanted to take this scene next. For example, did they want to push on with what this was doing to their friendship, or did they want to examine what was on Donna's mind that was making her not want to deal with Nakeisha? This led to an interesting conversation about friendship, drugs, and how girls deal with stress, until they felt ready to shoot their next scene.

Another scene involved 13 people, all of whom had enrolled themselves as part of an extended soap opera family. The soap opera setting created a safe space for these participants to interact with often painful stereotypes and identities on their own terms. In this particular scene, Jimmy, Colleen's son, was the only white person in the soap opera family. They all discussed how come this was so and how he felt about it. There was much comedy as they all tried to rationalize the situation, coming up with the idea that Jimmy was an adopted child in the family. Jimmy said that was fine; he was very happy to be in the family.

One of the other members of this extended soap opera family was, in real life, a drug dealer. He had enrolled himself as an *ex*-drug dealer, trying on a new persona, and was applauded for this new role. Yet another member chose to play a welfare officer, challenging the expected demographic of the role with self-reflective humor. And so it went. Amidst laughter and mischief, they came up with personal and institutional issues which they could discuss as actors, sometimes finding brilliant solutions.

The magic of this method of activating change was that it bypassed defenses and played to the strengths of the creative and humorous spirit, which under ordinary circumstances was habitually squashed or uninvited. Serious matters were raised and dissected, and many problems found solutions. In the end, these creative sessions brought to conscious awareness what were sometimes very painful issues.

Unfortunately, we were unable to study which acted events were transformed into personal change. The process was flourishing, but, alas, at the end of the year Matt left us to get married and moved away, and shortly afterward that housing project was dismantled for renovation. Before Matt left, we held a "film festival" pizza party in which the various soaps—some shorts, some connected in longer sequences—were screened in the community center.

We had, from the beginning, called our entire program in the housing developments FUN—Family Union Network. The absence of playful fun in these communities was so clearly evident that a good part of our work was to try to make things fun, to encourage free-spirited play. The soap opera was one such effort.

FAMILY CHOICES PROGRAM

Teen pregnancy was rampant in most low-income communities. We were interested in what it meant to teenage girls to have babies and to teen boys to make girls pregnant. While some of these pregnancies were accidental, many were consciously or unconsciously deliberate. David Kantor led a group of Family Center staff together with a community mental health clinic in Boston to explore reasons for this epidemic and to look for possible interventions.

The hypothesis behind this project was that girls get pregnant for a series of different reasons, many having to do with their relationships with their mothers. After identifying the "structures" we thought encouraged pregnancy, we used a visual and active intervention to try to bring awareness to a two-generation dyad of mothers and daughters—or more precisely, grandmothers, daughters who already had a baby, and their younger female siblings. We created a series of short videos, intentionally acted rather poorly by actresses and deliberately leaving much space for improvement, which depicted four critical family issues that might encourage pregnancy. They were: 1) Who wants the baby? 2) Who has the power to decide? 3) Mom's relationships with men. And, 4) Mom's influence on her children's sexual practice.

We invited families in to review the tapes and to give us advice as to how accurate they were and what could make them better. By putting families in control as film critics, they felt entitled to give their true opinions and to criticize the films. After the critique there was discussion of the issues as they applied to their actual families. One family enormously criticized a particular tape. They told us that they could show us what the themes in the tape were *actually* like in real life, and the next week they appeared with 16 people, complete with four toddlers, several young moms and dads, and some older mothers. They enacted a scene in front of the camera, having a good laugh as they went along, and proceeded to reproduce almost exactly what the original tape had shown. When the laughter died down and they realized how similar their rendering was to the original video, they began their first family-wide discussion of the subject of early pregnancies, and their meaning and implications for the family.

This was not a family that could communicate easily. We learned that Mom had serial boyfriends, all of whom in one way or another—through drug dealing, having guns in the house, or threatening family members—made the rest of the family feel unsafe. When any family member indicated disapproval of the new man Mom brought into the family, tensions arose. To counteract this, quite unconsciously, one of the teenagers would make noisy references to having more kids in the house—creating an alternative, distracting narrative. When David Kantor asked the family whether there was a connection between the conversations about Mom's men and all the young children and pregnant teens, one of the family members broke the code and said that this was always what happened when they brought up the new man threatening the safety of the family. After naming the connection, the family was able to begin an important conversation about a family pattern in which everyone had a part to play, all wanting things to change, and each move designed to keep the peace. It seemed safer to get pregnant than to get into a family fight.

For this family, this intervention enabled conversations to take place, safely and over time, where real relationship issues could be discussed and new patterns could be attempted where no one needed to get hurt. The intervention, along with family sculpture exercises, and various games about the decision to have a baby and whose responsibility it was, brought insights that were far from obvious, and which we hoped would produce collective decision-making. They were discovering their own strengths and resources together, and the developing sense of empowerment and possibility was impossible to miss.

6

PATTERNS

Getting Stuck

RETURNING TO CHARMAINE'S STORY, WE CAN SEE THE effects of perpetual stress and trauma on her ability to control her family and in some cases, her own impulses. Her drug use, which probably began as a form of self-medication, led to a constant habit and greatly impacted her ability to feed her family. Her traumatic history of sexual abuse as a young girl led to her being unable to protect her own daughter, and unable to draw boundaries of permissible behavior on the part of the men she brought into her house. An early invasion of one's personal space like this, and especially of one's own body, can create an imprint in the brain which says "anyone can invade my space, and I can't do anything about it."

As we have now seen from Charmaine's story and others, one of the devastating facts we learned while working in our original public housing developments was that childhood sexual assault was not unique. In almost every single family we worked with, sexual abuse was a salient component, and almost all of these abuses were involved with other types of domestic violence as well. That was 30 years ago. Much of this same situation persists today.

Charmaine was the head of her complex household, but she was not in control of it. And in her case, there was no one who could step in to help her out or take her place on a reliable basis. On top of all of this, she also had to cope with the realities of living in a dangerous neighborhood. Dangerous neighborhoods have everyone on alert. The high alert required to survive in such an environment inhibits normal brain development and diminishes a sense of future possibility. This means that children are less likely to do well in school, have fewer positive incentives from their parents, often fail to make the link between doing well in school and getting good jobs, and have difficulty maneuvering in relationships. When fear arises, it is likely to be converted instantly into violence or further withdrawal and isolation rather than being confronted, acknowledged, and managed. This holds true whether in family disagreements or in the larger contexts, where it can take the form of gang activity or group hostilities.

"In all cultures," Minuchin writes, "the family imprints its members with selfhood. Human experience of identity has two elements: a sense of belonging and a sense of being separate. The laboratory in which these ingredients are mixed and dispensed is the family, the matrix of identity."

Our families are our first and most basic "holding environment." They are the key unit in any community that provides support, nurturance, regulation, and socialization. They govern and mediate activities and feelings among their members and between their members and the larger community. Our families set our basic values and the rules for acting upon those values; they establish a set of expectations, and give us a sense of identity. If, as in Charmaine's case, the family is not functioning well, family members can become untethered and have difficulty finding ways through their many challenges just to survive.

Families organize themselves differently depending on who is there. In the nuclear family model, the family has two generations, comprising two parents and children. Sometimes grandparents live upstairs or nearby. While this is one kind of family structure, the families we work with have tended toward other organizational patterns.

In this chapter I describe four reoccurring characteristics and patterns of families whom we have known. These complex patterns, though not always as bleak as I've presented them here, were, to some degree, at the core of virtually every family we met in the housing projects, and to some degree have remained true for many of our client families since then.

FAMILY STRUCTURE

The first of these characteristics concerns family structure. Within many of these families the mother, like Charmaine or Colleen, is often the key resource. In this kind of family structure, families are often composed of members of three or four generations, and in 90% of these cases, the mother is the head of the household. There are often multiple fathers, but their presence is frequently, at best, fleeting; sometimes it is dangerous. Therefore, it is the mother who is most often the adult responsible for providing a secure environment in which her family can grow. Her freedom and capacity to provide elements of safety and nurturance are essential for the healthy development of all her family members.

In some cases, this mother can be a grandmother and a daughter in the household at the same time. She fits within a generational framework where she is not necessarily the eldest female, but where she is the designated head of household, with power to influence her children, her children's children, occasionally her great-grandchildren, and sometimes even her own parents. She is the hub of a complex web of relationships, some with people who may be only distantly blood-related or not related at all.

It is the mother's house, her territory. Her role gives her a mandate and a responsibility. Her values, the themes of her life, and the implicit rules for carrying them out permeates the atmosphere and affects everyone. People entering into Mom's space know what they can do and cannot do. They quickly learn how to operate within the family system, creating patterns of behavior geared to accommodate Mom's way of life, and rules of behavior for their own benefit. It is a one-party system. This is a key element of the organizational pattern. Without another head of household, a spouse or significant other, the mother's system goes unchallenged and unaided. You find your place within it or you leave, though you can return "on probation," or transiently. And there is often no one to share with the mother the family burdens and responsibilities unless she enrolls one of her children.

ATTACHMENT

The second area concerns relationships, specifically four ways parents and children attach to each other and the implications for each of these forms of attachment. People are programmed to seek relationships. Attachment theory tells us that the way early relationships develop can tell us a lot about how relationships in the future will manifest. We know that even though adults may remember early traumatic events, they often cannot remember the feelings of the trauma, or alternatively, when they can remember the feelings, they may not be able to relate them to actual events. These unprocessed traumas can commonly impede an adult's capacity to parent children in consistent and healthy ways. The children of parents with unprocessed traumas may fail in school or fail to make friends because of what Selma Fraiberg, in her seminal work "Ghosts in the Nursery," called "visitors from the unremembered past."

In the case of Charmaine and her daughter Mia, we are looking at a pattern of emotional disruption between mother and daughter that can be understood on several levels. Not only was there no healthy maternal role model for either to follow, but there was also damage for both women at the cellular level. Recent research tells us that brain development, especially for young children whose brains are developing at a rapid daily rate, can be sidetracked by the autonomic parts of the brain, which react to stress. While the autonomic parts of the brain are an essential element in all human beings that alert us to possible danger, when there is a chronic alarm going off, the continuous stress prevents other parts of the brain from fully developing.

These other parts of the brain constitute the "intentional self," governing physical, mental, and emotional development—skills related to self-regulation, empathy, curiosity, relationships, and concentration, among others. There are long-term consequences to disrupting development in these areas. When a child grows up under constant stress and fear, certain neural connections in the developing brain are damaged, making it harder for the child to form relationships, to be curious, or even to learn how to read. When this child becomes an adult, like Charmaine, the neural wiring that was so vital to surviving a childhood of familial—and often community—challenges, combines with the adult stressors associated with poverty, violence, racism, and possible addictions, to negatively affect a person's ability to self-regulate, plan, or make decisions.

They also impact a mother's ability to become emotionally attuned to the needs of her infant or growing child. The unprocessed or never discussed experiences in her past can impede her capacity to parent her children in consistent and healthy ways. It may mean she is likely to be inattentive to her child's cries, and later, to her daughter's stress. She might unwittingly exhibit an inability to protect her child in much the same way that she was left unprotected when she was threatened as a child. In a situation with secure attachment between parent and child, Charmaine would have been attuned to her daughter at every level of her development. But, as it was, her own childhood trauma had largely incapacitated her. Thus, there was a significant deficit in the quality of attachment in her relationship with her children.

Children become "securely attached" to their parents or caregivers when parents are sensitive and attuned to the cues of their infants. These parents are effective in understanding the cries of their infants, and can make sense of and respond to the moment-to-moment signals. The securely attached child develops good peer relationships in school, is more independent and able to explore the world more freely, is less vulnerable to stress, and is able to take advantage of opportunities. By contrast, non-securely attached infants, as they grow, have more difficulty achieving meaningful relationships.

There are three generally recognized categories of insecure attachment: avoidant, ambivalent, and disorganized. In avoidant attachment, the parent does not respond to the child's signals in a reliable way. As a consequence, the child becomes habituated to ignoring or avoiding the parent. Twenty-five years after her original study, follow-up studies of Dr. Mary Ainsworth's "Strange Situation"—which tested parent-infant attachment—found that adults who had been diagnosed as having avoidant attachment to their parents were restricted emotionally, aloof, controlling, and generally "unlikeable." Dr. Daniel Siegel found that many of these children, now adults, demonstrated disorientation, an unclear connection to others, and an inability to clear away chaos, with a tendency to dissociate.

The second category of insecure attachment, ambivalent attachment, refers to infants with parents who are inconsistent in their attunement and are often intrusive when they are present. These infants become children who are not easily soothed. They experience considerable anxiety and a pervasive sense of insecurity as adults. They have a difficult time finding a comfortable sense of self.

A distressing pattern of ambivalent attachment we often see in early emotional bonding is the mother who relates to the infant erratically, sometimes seeing the infant as a prized possession, sometimes as an alien object. The constancy of a healthy mother-child bonding is absent even though the mother may love the child very much. Without the early experience of being able to "count on" one's mother to be there, children grow up uncertain and insecure in their relationships. The mother, who may be not much more than a child herself, may not have received this kind of unconditional love and attention when she was a baby, and therefore does not have the resources within herself to engage securely with her own child. In this sense, it is a generationally inherited attachment deficit, and it is more than likely to continue into the next generation unless it is interrupted.

The third category, disorganized attachment, is the toughest, both to experience and to treat. It is estimated that 10% of the population experience this kind of attachment syndrome, but that 80% of families in high-risk populations have this kind of background. The common response of a child to this last category of disabling attachment is to fight, run away, or freeze— following the evolutionary set of responses built into our bodies as alarm systems that signal danger and prepare us to respond. What we choose to do depends on the type and level of danger we are sensing. If we can fight back, we will do so; if running away is a better option, we will run. If a small child is being beaten by an angry parent and cannot run away, he or she will freeze in place, trying to become invisible, and will also probably try to "mentally" escape such a frightening situation.

Colleen's story illustrates a pattern of disorganized attachment that affected her life and the lives of her children. Colleen had no idea what her children needed, as she herself had never had her own needs met as a child. She had no experiences to draw upon that might have informed her how to care for her own children. As we came to know her better, we learned that she, like so many others of our clients, had been sexually assaulted as a child. As a poor teenager living in a trailer park in North Carolina, she had been repeatedly raped by her father while her mother stood outside the trailer, helpless. Colleen had no capacity to make sense of her past or its effects on her relationships. Her "friends" were safe TV characters, and her children were just supposed to know what to do. When we first encountered her, her mode of relating to her children was continuous and frightening anger—it seemed as if in this behavior, she was beating back the ghosts of her own horrific past. Which, in fact, was precisely what she was doing.

As Daniel Siegel has noted, "The best predictor of a child's security of attachment is not what happened to his parents as children, but rather how his parents made sense of those childhood experiences." It was with this awareness—helping parents to make sense of their own childhood experiences, together with Selma Fraiberg's work on the need to remember the effect of the painful experience as well as the experience itself—that we built our programs. As Fraiberg once hypothesized about a family where the mother was unable to respond to her baby, "When the mother's cries are heard, she will hear her child's cries." The mother Fraiberg was referring to grew up in a gruesome world, not unlike Colleen's, where the family mantra aimed at any sort of pain was "Forget About It."

Colleen's resistance to hugging her son Jimmy, who so desperately needed love and affection, was an instance of her inability to directly show love. Colleen could not hug her child until she was taught how to put him in a tight "punishing" hold, what I was calling a "squeeze box," where hugging him was performed as a quasi-punishment. Both she and Jimmy knew it felt good, but they could not give it a soft name, a name that denoted love instead of anger.

With the confusion of affection and power messages such as this, it is not always possible to distinguish which one is really intended. A mother, for example, will want some connection with her child, but she may be afraid to get too close. She will yell as a way of keeping a sufficiently safe distance. In these ambiguous communications, sometimes people mistake what is intended, an authentic power communication—that is, a serious instruction about controlling behavior—or a gesture of affection. This creates difficulties for the mother in establishing boundaries and setting limits.

When there is ambiguity like this, mothers can feel helpless in having the impact they want. When the mother feels helpless, children experience a sense of power that is frightening. They do not know what to do with it or how to control themselves. They also then become enrolled as mother's mothers, which can lead eventually to panic. Colleen had lost control of her kids, and they reacted by creating terrible messes and hitting her. Her helplessness with her children was a less dangerous repeat of her own childhood experience with her mother. When she finally sought help for "parent abuse," Colleen's complaint against her children was a sign that she knew she had lost control; she was calling for help. In that sense, it was an indication of strength—a demonstration that her will to survive had not completely collapsed. Over time Colleen learned to be clearer about what she was feeling and thinking, which made it easier for her children to know what was going on and what was expected.

ENMESHMENT

The third of these patterns delves more deeply into a characteristic I call enmeshment. In the stages of healthy development, a child begins its life with a symbiotic attachment to its mother. It is utterly dependent, and mother and child are "inseparable." This stage, when successful, is referred to by Dr. D.W. Winnicott as the "bliss of oneness." Then, through the stages of growth, the child becomes increasingly separated and autonomous, developing a sense of identity, independence, and clear boundaries. As autonomy develops, so does the capacity for relationships and mutuality.

Many of our client families displayed a deviation from this healthy process of separation and individuation. The pattern which emerged was one in which a mother and child remained enmeshed as essentially one unit. Murray Bowen, a renowned family therapist, once noted that on visiting day at a pediatric inpatient unit, when the parents were more interested in the child than each other, after the visit, the child's condition would worsen. But when the parents connected well with one another, after the visit, the child's condition improved.

In enmeshed relationships, there is an insufficiently clear separation between mother and child, which can create a situation where the mother expects the child to know what *she* knows. At an unconscious level, the mother feels that she and her child are the same person. A "pseudo" bonding has occurred between parent and child, where the roles and position of each are, in a sense, indistinguishable. Instead of true nurturance and bonding, the two have become fused, and their communication patterns are also fused, and as such, are almost incomprehensible to an outsider. The mother may, for example, yell at a child, saying, "How many times have I told you not to climb on the hot stove?" Something that clearly would be an inappropriate expectation of a six-month-old! This form of communication breakdown leads, then, to difficulty in establishing boundaries and setting limits.

The mother's motives for having had this baby are likely to be complex. In many cases, the mother is young. She may have experienced failure in the outside world—done poorly in school or been unable to find a good job. Where she may have failed to be creative in earlier parts of her life, there is the sense that in motherhood, she can express a potentially unfettered creative impulse and feel wholly satisfied. She may experience the world as unpredictable and insecure, without a place she can call her own or a person whom she can count on. The baby may be viewed as a stabilizing element, someone she can love and someone to love her. In some cases, she may have been losing ground socially among her peers by not becoming pregnant; the baby will correct this. For many, motherhood provides a valid and culturally sanctioned identity.

She may also have motives related to her own mother. She may be struggling for some lost or never fully gained attention from her mother, and the new baby may be a kind of gift to her mother in exchange for this hoped-for attention. Or in other cases, the young mother may be unhappily dependent on her own mother and struggling for the feeling and recognition of independence. In this case, the baby may feel like her only way to become separate and achieve "adult" status, or a kind of pseudo-adulthood. Other reasons may be that the family is "depressed," with its adolescent and adult members living apparently without hope or purpose. Here, the baby will liven things up and provide something positive to focus on. Or the girl may simply want to emulate her mother and want to carry on the family's tradition.

Regardless of motive, in all of these situations, the baby is perceived by the young mother as a necessity and as her possession, rather than being seen as an independently viable person. As long as the baby developmentally remains passively dependent, it carries out this function. But when the baby or child makes a significant gesture toward independence, a crisis is created.

There are critical periods when these crises are likely to occur. The first stage occurs around six months of age when the baby becomes mobile. Developmental milestones are met and experienced with mixed feelings in all families, but for this mother, the fact that the baby can move on its own is a threatening experience. She thinks of her baby as her wholly controlled possession, and all of a sudden, she can no longer control it absolutely. Most mothers want their children to grow and thrive, but they also want to keep that sense of oneness. This mother may celebrate the child's beginning mobility but may also simultaneously feel a sense of loss and foreboding. Meanwhile, the newly mobile baby has its own ideas about where it wants to go, and that movement may be away from Mom. Instead of welcoming this indication of growth toward independence, the mother can become frightened and angry, often attributing to the child malevolent motives and sophisticated understanding. In this relationship, at the moment when the baby physically moves away, it is in danger of being rejected, and another baby may be conceived to "replace" it.

The second period where the move toward independence can be critical occurs as the child gets ready to go to school for the first time. Here the mother experiences the same anxieties, but she is now focused on the school system that threatens to accelerate the separation process, taking her child away for parts of each day. The school intervenes in her relationship with the child, challenging the mother's definition of it and imposing a new one. It is possible, then, even at this early stage, that the mother begins an unconscious undermining process with respect to school, perceiving as she does that its intentions and hers are in conflict.

The third period when a move toward independence confronts an enmeshed parent-child relationship is during early adolescence. By this time, the child has sought independent recognition for 13 or more years. The mother-child relationship is fraught with strains. The mother may attempt to reject the child, or at least ignore the palpable needs for love and guidance, by now so well disguised. She is vulnerable, undifferentiated from her child, not being able to create an autonomous sense of herself. Rather, she is dependent on continual connection to her children to maintain the sense of her own fragile identity. If asked what her aspirations are, she is not likely to have any. She is more likely to have aspirations for her children. The child may become the bearer of hopes which the mother no longer dares to have for herself. When her own dream vanished, it was transferred to the next generation.

As the child goes through adolescence, the mother may feel of no use to the child, whom she may abandon emotionally altogether and even expel from the house. She may alternate between blaming herself and her child. She may struggle to deliver mature messages to her child, but is then likely to take them back and thus undermine her own effectiveness. She cannot take in the contextual realities of the child's life as an autonomous person. She cannot help herself consolidate her identity and move forward.

She projects her frustration as anger onto the child, and then will back off, often acquiescing to whatever decisions the child comes up with—a behavioral pattern which frequently validates and encourages precisely what she fears.

Beneath the anger that she is likely to express is often remorseful sadness for herself and for her child. Her identity as a mother is all she's got, and it is failing her. For children, this is a painful time. Their mother appears to be abandoning them just when they need her most, when they are grappling with peer pressures, life decisions, hormone rushes, and a changing body. The children are getting no direction. This fragile relationship, where children have never felt truly seen, listened to, or understood because of the enmeshed quality of the mother-child bonding, is taking a turn for the worse. Rather than engaging a child, the mother is letting go. Taking this cue, the child may leave home abruptly, sometimes with nowhere to go.

During this adolescent period, if the child is a daughter, she may become pregnant to unconsciously repeat the enmeshment cycle. She also may experience competition from her mother for boyfriends, as well as over her physical appearance. The mother's boyfriend may be taken with the daughter and may make advances on her. Since the boundaries have never been distinct in the enmeshed relationship, it is not unusual for the mother to "permit" such crossing of the lines while also resenting it. Likewise, it is not unusual for the daughter's boyfriend and the mother to develop a "special" relationship. Mother and daughter can collude around this competition, sometimes becoming "best friends" and, alternately, rivals.

For a boy child, this period of young adolescence is also a crisis point, although there appears to be less strain in this regard between mother and sons than with daughters. However, two characteristic patterns often can occur. In one, the son must struggle to leave home, often having to do so in an aggravated fashion. Where the son is struggling to leave, he experiences ambivalent feelings and thus moves back and forth, often experimenting for short periods of time outside the home, sometimes acting badly, and at times even being expelled by his mother or forced out by the courts. This exercise in autonomy is tumultuous and establishes a pattern likely to recur at a later age when the son may be in and out of the home of a significant other.

In the other pattern, the mother and son collude to keep the son home as her "pseudo" partner, even after he has reached maturity. The mother often makes weak threats to put him out if he doesn't find a job, but doesn't act on them. Her son is useful to her as a man in the house, both to help care for other children and as protection from other men. It is also a way the mother can protect her son from the very real threats to his survival on the street. Even though while she is doing this, she is also potentially disabling him from becoming competent in performing effectively in the world.

In enmeshed families, the enmeshment generally runs throughout the system. The roles and boundaries of all the family members become indistinct and overlapping. The parents share with children intimacies that are more usually reserved for adults. The children are conscripted into adult responsibilities of running the family, and the adults become childlike by having their authority prematurely usurped. The confusion of affective and power messages is one kind of communication failure that occurs. But the main characteristic has to do with the failure to recognize the "other" as "other." In a truly enmeshed situation, there is no "other"; there are only extensions of one's self or one's self as an extension of another.

SEXUAL ABUSE

The fourth and final of these characteristics deals specifically with the prevalence and effects of sexual abuse and assault. In many of these families, patterns of abuse and victimization started early, usually in childhood. Often the abuser was a father or other relative, or sometimes a mother's boyfriend or a family friend. When this intrusive act occurs at an early age, it becomes embedded in the psyche, with the power to order meaning and ways of perceiving subsequent experiences. The lives and actions of survivors are sifted through this filter. While these survivors can be any member of the family—female, male, or other gender identities—they are most often female.

A common pattern we saw in relation to sexual abuse took the shape of a victimized/victimizing triangle. Charmaine's daughter Mia's experience can be pictured using this triangle. There are usually three people involved in the act of child abuse—the abuser, the abused, and the powerless bystander. The abuser, in this case, Joey Sr., had almost all the power. Charmaine, the girl's mother, was disempowered because of the abuse she herself experienced at the same age, and was unable to protect her daughter. The daughter, Mia, unprotected by her mother, was direct prey for the abuser.

This complex, highly charged experience of abuse is at the core of the survivor's traumatic memory picture. The person who perpetrates this act on an innocent child is likely to be male, and is likely to have been a victim of physical (and sometimes also sexual) abuse as a child who is now reenacting his experience in the role of the perpetrator. He may be enmeshed or semi-enmeshed with his mother, may be in and out of the life of a significant other like Charmaine, may not be receiving the recognition and gratification that he craves, and may be frightened of making commitments on a more adult level. The mother of the abused child was most likely, as we have seen in Charmaine's case and others, sexually or physically abused herself. She established through that experience a sense of herself as someone to whom things are done, outside of her control. Most profoundly, she learned that she is a person who engages in relationships where victimization is the constant currency. She will tend to repeat the victimizing pattern in all her relationships, and her daughter may have been taught to do the same. In some cases, the child's mother, if she is the abuser's lover, may also be unconsciously directing him toward the girl.

Many mothers living in these environments are also victimized by the culture of poverty that eats away at them. As one mother put it, ". . . after that [school failure], there's nothing else to do but to have a baby and, you know, try and get some help to help you support it and build your own home, 'cause that's the only way out for a woman." She tends to blame herself for her failure to "make it" according to the rules and values of middle-class America. Society, social organizations, and demeaning racism may have colluded to disempower her and contributed to her status of helpless victim.

This stance of "victim" is not uncommon among women across socioeconomic classes. Throughout history, women have been coerced into accepting passive, receptive, and accommodating roles, and have therefore been easy targets for abusive behavior. But with consciousness comes resistance and the power to change.

Understanding the intricacies of how these patterns worked, both alone and interactively, helped us design interventions to block generational transmission, and to alleviate at least in part some of the pain they caused the families we knew and came to love. The people who survived these challenges have strengths others do not, and one cannot underestimate the positive and strong patterns that were also present in these families. Those strengths were what they hung onto, and how they managed what, to some of us, might seem unimaginable.

Along with strength, there was also joy in these families, and the capacity to grow. With nurturing and coaching, these parents developed healthier habits for themselves and their families and learned to become more attuned to themselves and to their children.

7

ACTION TECHNIQUES

"The First 40 Years of Parenthood Are Always the Hardest"

AS THE FAMILY CENTER CAME INTO ITS OWN AS AN ORGANI-
zation, we were increasingly aware that we were carving
out a unique place at the intersection of psychoeducation,
trauma-informed family support, family therapy, and social justice. We were "universal," addressing issues relevant to any parent, and did not require or look for a mental health diagnosis.
This nonpathological orientation gave us the power to destig-
matize therapy while still providing a therapeutic experience.
We weren't targeting specific symptoms, and we didn't regard
our programs as specifically educational or behaviorally focused.
The niche we occupied enabled distressed and sometimes very
disturbed parents to understand things about themselves without feeling judged or labeled, and then to change some critical

behaviors, breaking painful generationally inherited patterns. The purposeful mix of parents who might have different diagnoses (or none at all) and varied life experiences, including different ethnic, racial, and class backgrounds, provided us with a rich community of people sharing basic human predicaments.

In our first 15 years, our small staff of 17, mainly working in the projects, learned the fundamentals about what people were experiencing, about their attitudes toward their lives, about their perceptions of us and ours of them. We learned about interventions that worked and ones that didn't. As we decided to move on to other communities and expand our reach, we found that many of the interventions we had developed worked well in a group format, and we brought those together in a new structure. That new structure was Parenting Journey.

Among the psychodrama, gestalt, storytelling, and other expressive therapies, we counted more than 30 action-oriented interventions—in a varied, experiential core curriculum. Family therapy interventions did not fit as precisely—although the theoretical foundation remained sound—so we also developed a companion program to Parenting Journey called Family Coaching/Family Campaign for individual families following participation in Parenting Journey programs. The Family Coaching curriculum contained many of the Parenting Journey features, and allowed families to practice new behaviors with their newly learned insights. This chapter discusses a few of the Parenting Journey interventions, all of which include the notions of respect, strength, self-efficacy, and collaboration.

JOINING

When we attempt to "help" others, we are unlikely to be successful unless we form a safe relationship. As helpers, we are not outside the emotional system of our clients; we are a part of it. Systems of relationship intertwine between mother and child, other family members, friends, and community—as well as helping institutions. Not infrequently, helping institutions do not adequately recognize the importance of their role in these systems. Too often the relationship between helper and client takes the form of a hierarchical arrangement, where the helper has explicit or implicit control over the ones being helped. Sometimes the control is stark, as when an agency has the power to decide whether a child must be taken into foster care or be allowed to live with his or her parents. But stark or subtle, helpers commonly clothe themselves in an aura of knowing more, and shepherding the client—a family, for example—in the direction which the helper has decided is best.

What happens then? The family might rebel, slam the door as Charmaine did on the Department of Social Services officer, or passively resist and refuse to engage with the helper or the helper's ideas. There might be monosyllabic "yeses," perhaps indicating assent, or more likely attempts to please the helper sufficiently to hurry him or her out of the house. The helper in this situation begins to feel helpless, and may react to that helplessness by asserting him or herself more forcefully, trying to persuade the family of the rightness of his/her position. The downward spiral begins with the family feeling threatened or at the very least disrespected and the helper, becoming increasingly annoyed, pressing on. The family members are saying to themselves, or perhaps even out loud, "You don't know my life, my values, what I've been through. You think you know, but you don't. I don't want to listen to you. I know what to do (or maybe I don't, but I won't tell you)." With this, the helper and the client have become antagonists, and everyone involved knows it.

We learned very quickly to take a different approach. We were aware that when we came into someone else's home, Charmaine's, for example, we were on *her* turf, not ours. We were respectful. We took a one-down position, like Columbo, the bumbling television detective I so admired in my childhood. The fact is, we *were* know-nothing bumblers, intruding into unknown and complicated territory.

Often mental health professionals or child welfare workers feel they have to know more—or act as if they know more—than they actually do. But what if they don't have to pretend any longer? What if they can be respectful, curious interlopers for a few minutes into someone else's world? They can actually be themselves. They don't need the shield of "professional conduct" or the memes of "proper boundaries." Professional distance is not always a protection. Instead of being the one in control, another way is to become a partner in the search. Many of our staff came from families like those they were encountering, and thus they had more implicit knowledge than others with different backgrounds. We all had something to teach and something to learn.

In Nadia's story, we saw how her sharing her own experience of sexual abuse brought her closer to the daughters and mothers in the group she was leading. They could trust her because they knew she understood. And they knew they were all in it together. When you share something personal, you have the attention of the others in the room. When you do this as a group leader, you are doing something else as well. You are acknowledging that you are not the know-it-all leader; you are another person who is also on a journey. You have reduced the hierarchy between the leader and the clients. You are leading from the side—walking the walk together.

In one of our first Parenting Journey meetings, the group leader (or facilitator as they are called) noticed that one woman in the group had not opened her mouth. It was the fourth session, and she hadn't said a word. Why? Exasperated and trying to draw the woman out, the facilitator grabbed a mirror. "I look in the mirror," she told the group, "and I know this face is bright and intelligent, but it's too fat. My mama always told me I was too fat, so I look at that face, and I see fat. I don't see beauty or intelligence." When she stopped, the silent woman cleared her throat and, softly at first, said she was told the same thing; she felt the same way. That broke the ice; after that she didn't have a problem talking. Just as it had been with Nadia, this episode was another lesson that told us that sharing something of ourselves with the group could make the group environment safer, and made us more human and alike, and easier to trust. It pushed the group forward.

Understanding our place and sharing our experiences are ways of joining with our clients. And in order to help in any kind of mental health or social welfare capacity, one needs to join. "Joining," in the sense that Salvador Minuchin meant it, involves genuinely connecting with someone, feeling some kind of mutuality, and at least a modicum of trust.

For clients who have had bad histories of trauma, this is not easy. They are, as we know, on their guard every moment, their alarm systems ready to go off. How does one diffuse this self-protecting alarm mechanism? One way is to join in telling stories, finding daily human experiences we all encounter. "You have a 9-year-old son throwing things around the house and yelling at the top of his lungs? So do I." Or joining can be through action: "Shall we go to the grocery store together? Why don't we shop together? Then I can get my stuff as well, and I can drive you home."

In one Parenting Journey group, Donna, an immigrant from Guatemala, walked into the large room where the table had been set for a group dinner, place mats on the table, candles and plastic flowers in the center. She put both hands to her cheeks in surprise. "Nobody ever set a table for me before, not in my whole life!" she said. She felt respected and welcomed.

One cannot emphasize enough how important starting off with a respectful attitude is in forming a solid relationship. For so long, many families stuck in the welfare system, demeaned by racism, enmeshed in immigration efforts, those who have been rocked by abuse or violence, or in fact, any troubled family at all, have often been treated disrespectfully and blamed for their situation as if they had willingly created it. They are in fact twice cursed—first by the circumstance they have come to be in, and second, by a helper who lets on, sometimes subtly, that the family has brought this on itself and now it is time to pay. When the table is set, with candles and flowers, our client feels the caring and respect that will permit joining in a relationship.

Another challenge is to get around defenses. People who have been subjected to violence and abuse typically build walls around themselves. They are conditioned to fear that there is something they have not done right, that they will be punished for in some way if they are found out. One of our group members, Alicia, worried that she couldn't tell the truth about her crippling depression after the death of her 3-year-old child, who was run over by a truck. She had felt frozen since that happened and hadn't been able to care for her other children as she wanted to. Now the authorities were on her case. If she told them how depressed she was, how immobilized, would they take her kids away? She thought they might. She tried to appear strong and put together, the opposite of how she actually felt.

At Parenting Journey, Alicia showed up apprehensive, expecting to be challenged and blamed. Instead, the group facilitator welcomed her and asked her to look at an array of buttons spread out on a table in the therapy room. The buttons had short messages on them. "Pick one that appeals to you," the group facilitator said, "and put it on."

Most of the button messages were humorous, but with serious connotations: "Are a few dull moments too much to expect?" "Queen of the Bad Girls." "Born to Party, Forced to Work." "I'm not a nag; I'm a motivational speaker." "The complaint department is closed!" "The first 40 years of parenthood are always the hardest." "Doomed love affairs are my hobby." "Looking for a man to sweep me off my feet and then clean the rest of the house." "Tough times don't last, tough people do."

Alicia picked "The first 40 years of parenthood are always the hardest." When the group session started, the facilitator asked why she had chosen that button. Alicia told the group she had picked it because it was so hard for her to get anything done. She was constantly tired, and always seemed to give up before she finished anything. She knew her children noticed. She knew that even though they were young, they felt they had to take over the household. She felt like a failure.

The fact that everyone in the group was wearing a button, and each, obviously, had its own story, eased her discomfort about opening up. Everyone had similar stories to tell. The quasi-humorous button had allowed Alicia to tell a sensitive and painful story, at least in outline. Had she been asked directly how she was feeling, she would have said something like, "Fine, thank you." These interventions helped get beyond the psychological defenses that often make people feel safer but tend to block important awarenesses.

Another member had picked up a button that read "Queen of the Bad Girls." She described how she had been a junkie for 20 years and had messed up her life and her family's life. She wanted to change, but "I know how to be a bad girl," she said. "It can be fun." Another woman, Tamika, had chosen "The complaint department is closed." And in fact, she was determined to get rid of the problems holding her back and to do things that would make her life better. The button messages made people laugh, which further eased the process. The implications in their choices were serious, but laughing together was bonding and fun. Having fun is itself a joining experience, and a healing one.

SPECIAL OBJECTS

Curiosity is another attribute of "joining." When someone is curious about you, you feel attended to; you're being recognized. It makes you feel more interested and alive. Someone seems to care. When our groups start, people share their names and something about the origins of the name. Who named you? Who are you named after? A little bit of history begins to come out. In addition, you have been asked to bring a special object, something you really care about, or perhaps a photograph that reveals a significant piece of your personal history. You tell a story about the object, why it is important to you, what it means to you today, how it still affects you, and maybe even how it affects your parenting.

The "special objects" intervention came directly from Nadia's foundational mother-daughter group. While the group was meeting, some of the mothers in the group had brought objects that reminded them of their own mothers and how poorly they had taught them about the facts of growing up. One woman brought a pin that belonged to her mother. She explained that her mother was very vain, that she was always dressing up to go out and often wore this pin. She talked about how her mother was not interested in teaching her anything about sex or other aspects of growing up but instead was focused on looking in the mirror, admiring herself, and then disappearing. This now, in the telling, made her angry at how her mother had neglected her. She had never thought of it that way before, or how it might be playing out with her own daughter, how little she had communicated with her child about things *she* needed to know.

Charles, a member of another Parenting Journey group, was a powerfully built man in his forties. He brought in a pair of old work boots. He described how they were worn and battered, like he felt he was himself. But they had gotten him to his construction jobs, to his AA meetings when he was homeless, and to a better life now when he took his children for walks in the country.

Suzanna brought to her group a little bear that had belonged to her youngest child. He was 2 years old when the Department of Children and Families (DCF) took him for adoption. Her face was wet with tears as she remembered this child, who had loved the bear, as she had loved him. She was still too damaged by abuse and self-denigration to be able to consistently give this baby the kind of attention he needed. She would have fits of screaming about abandoning him, and about "hating herself." No matter how hard Suzanna tried and how much more she understood about the damaging effects of these fits to herself and her child, she could not control herself; the bad memories came back—her devil clawing at her. She had passed over to the numbed stage where she felt virtually nothing, and now was beginning to grapple with her untold ghosts.

These stories around special objects are all emotional in one way or another, either good or bad. They can be humorous and uplifting or tragic, sometimes hard to hear. Often, they are deep; some of them banal. But they are all human. These are people in a room with other people, sharing intimate things about their lives, joining with each other and helping ease each other's problems.

CREATING SAFETY

A critical tool in a group setting is setting rules and boundaries. Rather than the leader coming in with a ready-made list, in Parenting Journey groups, group members make their own rules. A blank chart is affixed to a board. Group members trace their handprints on the chart with colored pencils, placing them in a circle. They are then asked to write in each outlined finger qualities that they will contribute to the group. Then they read them aloud. This exercise literally places their imprint on the group, and expresses qualities they have to offer. Then the group together calls out characteristics that they want to see in the group. They discuss each one, and must come to agreement before it becomes one of the "rules" of the group. This invites people to disagree and shows in a light way how disagreement can be useful and enhance group clarity as well as sharpen an individual's own thinking.

Someone might, for example, call out, "Trust." Someone else might ask for clarification. Another might say, "Nice idea, but we can't agree to trust each other; we don't even know each other." This might lead to a discussion of what we actually mean by trust. Can you trust in different ways? Can you trust someone to take your kids to school, but not trust them with a personal secret? Can you trust someone to show up at work on time but not trust them to cook a decent meal? Trust can come to be seen as way too comprehensive and vague. Chances are they'll come up with a substitute, something they all can agree on.

There are certain rules that must be applied for safety, and the facilitator can enforce them if they have not already been mentioned by the group—things like confidentiality and being a mandated reporter. But these will be fleshed out and clearly explained. For a population of people who mainly feel traumatized and with very little power in their lives, this exercise is a message that says, "Here you have control of your group. It is you, not someone else, who governs what goes on here. The characteristics of the group are defined by you, the group's members." As well as identifying the characteristics they want to see in the group, the group's members also brainstorm what sorts of characteristics they do not want to see in their group. Again, it must all be by mutual consent.

With the contract and constraints made by the group itself, the group becomes a powerful force of support for its members, and puts them in the driver's seat. Behaving according to their own devised rules, members are considerate, interested, and supportive of each other, and because of their diversity (no group is composed of homogeneous people with respect to ethnicity, race, class, problem, or other distinguishing features), they have a greater chance of aiding each other in problem solving and mutual encouragement, bringing different perspectives and life experiences. The group rules are posted at every session and are used by anyone in the group if they feel something is being violated.

The very fact of having a diverse group has another impressive impact on its members. A consequence of a diversely constituted group has been that members who are sometimes prejudiced or racist come to love and respect the very people from whom they initially differed the most or about whom they held the most critical views. The effect of this is that people trust what each has to say to the other precisely because they had such different starting points. One group member who also happened to have had an outside therapist said, "When someone in this group says I'm a good person or that I've done well, I believe them, and it feels much better than when my therapist says the same thing. She's paid to say these things. You aren't." The group becomes, de facto, a kind of family striving to become whole. It is far less frightening to look at aspects of one's past, sometimes reactivating old trauma, with a whole group than to do this work alone. Individuals have a room full of support to help them disconfirm the meanings of old memories and to help change those meanings into viable stories they can live with. Thus, the groundwork is laid for exploring real, concrete personal development.

RITUAL QUESTIONS

Once the rules are set, every group session begins with four "ritual questions." These are, in a sense, warm-up exercises.

Each question asks for a response that involves an actual experience. Taken together, the questions represent all of the fundamental elements in the program: they focus on caring for oneself, on communication, on strengths, and on personal awareness. These questions teach people about becoming mindful—paying attention to various aspects of themselves and others.

The first question is: "Name something you did for yourself this week." Interestingly, this is often the most difficult for our clients to answer. In the beginning they often can't think of a thing. It has a jolting effect. We give them a small notebook to take home so they can jot down something they did for themselves. It focuses attention in a new direction, saying, "You are worth paying attention to." A follow-up to this question is, "How did doing something for yourself affect your parenting?" We are making a connection here: having something for yourself, which then enables you to give to your children. It is like gassing up your car.

An answer to the first question might be: "I got my hair and nails done," or "I took a day to relax." Tamika said, "I cleaned and decluttered my house to start a new beginning." Suzanna said, "I spent the weekend in bed."

Often, but not always, the answers to this question become deeper as the discussions continue. Group members begin to rethink what the meaning of self-care is for them—from getting nails done, to exercising, to meeting and being with friends, to looking for a new job. The definition of self-care changes as there is an expanded awareness of what it feels like to be focusing on what one needs and deserves. Focusing is becoming mindful. This is often the first time many of the participants have ever experienced focusing on what they themselves need and deserve.

Their habitual manner may well be doing things that do not, in fact, benefit them.

The second question is: "Tell us a good conversation you had with someone this week." Here we are focused on relationship, communication, and the importance of an "other" in one's life. It alerts people to think about how they communicate, whether they are being coherent, how they are getting through, whether they're successful at this, and if not, why not. It shows them they have an ability they may not have thought they had. We can congratulate them and point out what was good about the conversation, about which they may not be completely aware. Examples of this often are, "I didn't shout at my daughter (or the child welfare worker who has custody of my child). I asked polite questions." Or, "With my child, I asked her what was on her mind. Was something troubling her? Had I done something that upset her?" The group leader can then follow up with a question, "How did it work out?" And usually you will get a positive, often surprised, answer.

When someone is asked to describe something good, they are energized and begin to feel better about themselves. Sometimes they have to dig deep to find this good conversation. It may be not so much that there were no good conversations, but rather that the group member was unaware that she had had such a conversation. She is used to "failing," trying to speak to someone and ending up shouting or slamming the door. That might be her more usual mode, and our challenge is to unearth a more successful approach. As we move farther along in the group's sessions, the conversations almost always become more nuanced and longer.

The third question is: "Describe a situation which you handled well that you are proud of." This builds on the previous question but includes more than a conversation. It involves thinking through a difficult challenge, making choices, taking responsibility, sticking with a situation until it is resolved. It implies that people have agency, which they may be unaware of, that they can manage, and afterward articulate what happened. Articulating a successful, challenging situation is like exercising an atrophied muscle. Many people do not think they can do it. When they find they can, it can come as a great "aha" moment—a sense of real accomplishment.

Interestingly, parents almost never bring up insubstantial issues. It's always something that matters to them. When Suzanna's best friend died, she held it together. She did not become violent or start cursing. She "held on" and was proud of how she handled the great loss of her friend, calling the friend's sister, going to her house. She had, by chance, dropped her phone that day and cracked the screen, but she didn't let that drive her into a fury of frustration, different from another time recently when she broke a brand-new TV in an uncontrollable outburst.

Tamika had a successful encounter with her children's uncle, who had custody of her children, looking good and "doing what she had to do" to make the difficult relationship between them work. While she wanted to criticize him and yell at him, she restrained herself, unlike other times when the uncle pushed her buttons (which he often did) and she exploded. Another young woman met a friend who told her how well her children in foster care were doing without her. "It broke my heart," she said. "But I had to take it in and move on."

The fourth question is: "Name a situation that you think you could have handled better." Originally this question was added because participants were so full of problems they wanted to discuss each week that we were unable to proceed with the program. When people are given a space, albeit a small one, to articulate a pressing issue, they think carefully ahead of time about the problem and about how they have been handling it before presenting it to the group. As a growing sense of safety develops in the group, members are more able and willing to share situations they could have handled better or differently. By the time they bring the problem to the group, they often have a better solution in mind. The process of filtering a complex issue has taken place in a more structured and thoughtful way. Gaining some distance from oneself, and searching for a possible alternative, is a significant learning experience. After this they are better able to seek help from the group, many of whom may have gone through similar experiences.

When individuals do seek advice from the group, there are several structured ways the facilitator might respond to this request. Let's say Sandra says that she got into a terrible fight with her daughter, who had disobeyed her and stayed out all night. The girl defended herself by saying it was none of her mother's business. Sandra disagreed, but the girl remained stubborn. Then the girl began to insult her mother and yell at her. Sandra slapped her in the face. The girl became more incensed and slammed out of the house.

Sandra came to group feeling desperate. Some of the questions we might ask are: a) "Did hitting her work?" Answer: "No"; b) "How did it make you feel, hitting your daughter?" Answer: "Really bad, losing my control like that, but it also was kind of a relief"; c) How were you punished when you disobeyed your parents? Answer: "The same way. They always hit me. I know it doesn't work, not with a stubborn person like me, and not with my daughter. But it's the only way I know"; d) To the group: "Does anyone have a thought about how else this situation could be resolved? Have any of you been in similar situations?"

At this point the group is brought in to search for an alternative, but only after the three other questions exploring the mother's experience have been discussed. Becoming aware of what is not working helps open up one's mind to new ideas. Asked how Sandra feels about all this, she says, "I see what you're saying. I do the same old stuff, and it doesn't work in the same old way. But it's all I know how to do. I'm glad to hear other people's experiences. Maybe that will make me think differently."

We can see how the mother is making the connection between her own experience as a child and her child's experience. The group begins to problem solve, reasoning things out together, and together coming up with some other possible approaches. One suggestion is that Sandra could share with her daughter how she felt when she was a teenager, and what might have helped her—what she had wished for but never dared ask. After considerable discussion, the group decides to do a role play, suggesting that Sandra pretend she is a representative of all mothers (thus loosening the sense of personal incompetence) and asking for a volunteer to be the daughter. Sandra then asks her "daughter" to tell her why she stayed out. But now she has the benefit of the group's discussion, and Sandra tries something different from the shouting and slapping that actually took place. What can she, she asks her daughter, do to make the daughter's life at home more comfortable?

The process of going through the four questions identifies areas to look at that many of our clients don't immediately think about. But these are not strange or onerous questions. On the contrary, they're ordinary and familiar; they provide a kind of safe base. Every group member can answer them at the depth at which they feel comfortable.

MEDITATION

The first question: "Name something you did for yourself this week" leads to reflection on what it means to take care of yourself. One kind of self-care we introduce is guided meditation. In several places in the Parenting Journey curriculum, group members attempt to change their current environment literally and imaginatively. They relax, the lights are dimmed, they close their eyes and are guided through relaxation exercises—noticing where they are tense, trying to release the tensions. Then they are asked to imagine a safe place they know of, to picture it in their minds. Later on, they will be asked to return to their safe place and imagine what life might be like with all their troubles removed, who might be with them and where they might be going from there, physically and emotionally. This part of the meditation exercise appears later in the curriculum, where they are focused on change.

The self-care aspect of this series of mindful meditations allows people to relax, glimpse something they may not have done before or might be afraid to imagine, on either a physical or psychological level. In the context of a group meditation, it feels safe to experience new things, to dream, to imagine, to play out a different game. This elaborates on elements of surprise, positivity, and creative spirit that, at some level, dwell within each human being.

8

GHOST STORIES

"Tough Times Don't Last, Tough People Do"

"How much one forgets but still lives with it anyway—
like a phantom limb."
—Elizabeth Strout

As Dr. Daniel Siegel suggests, what makes a critical difference in a person's development is not so much what happened to individuals as children but rather how individuals make sense of their experiences as adults. By telling your story to another, no matter how horrific or confusing, you begin to have it make sense to you. Pieces come together and are corroborated by the telling and by the response of others. One way Parenting Journey gets to this is by asking each participant to remember back, perhaps by imagining they are flipping through a photo album or just closing their eyes and focusing as they listen to an instruction. This instruction is simple: "Think of a time in your earlier childhood that was important to you for some reason. The reason can be a joyful occasion, a scary occasion, or a sad one. Close your eyes if you want to, and see that experience as a picture. Then pick up a crayon and draw this memory picture." When participants have drawn their pictures, they are asked to show them to the group, and by turn, tell the story that the picture represents. An image emerges involving early memory, perhaps almost forgotten. Once the picture is real and tangible on a piece of paper, it is easier to talk about it.

The second part of the exercise is to ask another group member to take a turn repeating back to the storyteller, as exactly as possible, everything they have heard, without questions or comments. If a part is forgotten, another member can jump in to finish it until the storyteller feels completely heard. By feeling heard, the story feels more coherent to the teller, and richer for having been shared.

The picture that Tamika drew was devastating. It depicted her mother being murdered by her stepfather while Tamika and her three younger siblings held hands and looked on. This drawing covered the very bottom part of the page. Above it she drew many clouds with a word in each one: "violence," "sad," "hurt," "upset," "knife," "court," "terrified," "alone," "scared," "confused." In another box on the lower right-hand side of the page, Tamika wrote "birthday," "anniversary," "date of death," all crossed out with heavy lines. Next to that and under the clouds, was the sad face of a little girl, tears coming down, dripping off the page.

Tamika explained her story. When she was 11 years old, her mother, to whom she was very close, was attacked and stabbed to death by her then-husband. The proximate cause was that

Tamika, the eldest of four children, refused to call her stepfather "Dad." As she described this story, she teared up, saying she felt it was her fault that her mother died, and she has never gotten over it. There would be much more later on about her relationship to her mother, but this particular memory anchored her in time and affect—a kind of "before and after" of her life. It is to this day the key image that guides her.

By holding the image physically in her hand, Tamika had exerted a certain control over her story, and when she heard that same story repeated back, it gave her a sense of being grounded and connected rather than being subjected to a deep, unexpressed trauma, helpless and alone. An indication of the power the group's participation had for her was that toward the end of the session, she said she felt "separation anxiety" from the group and wanted to figure out a way for them all to stay connected in the future.

The author Roger Rosenblatt says of stories, "In the first place, in the last place. That is what we people do—write messages to one another. We are a narrative species. We exist by storytelling, by relating our situations. And the test of our evolution may lie in getting the story right."

Groups sometimes feel uncomfortable not being able to express their feelings upon hearing a story such as this. I even needed to be convinced that this was the most fruitful way of eliciting sometimes fraught childhood stories. But our experience tells us that the capacity to listen and to just be present for another person has a strong effect. This is often the first time one of our parents has had the opportunity to stand before a group of people and be the center of attention. The parent feels important and is, at that moment, in control of the group. Secondly, the exercise of repeating back as exactly as possible what you have heard, without comment or opinion, helps distinguish between a fact and a point of view or analysis. And starting with the easy, childlike act of crayon drawing creates a powerful baseline for later storytelling.

The art of listening, communicating that you have heard the story, unadorned with your feelings, is powerful in all cultures. A woman had fled to Tanzania from her native Burundi, which was experiencing a ferocious civil war. While in Tanzania she had gotten married and then divorced and had contracted AIDS. When she returned to Burundi, she was ashamed of what had happened to her and had not told anyone of her condition. By drawing a picture of herself crossing the border, sick and afraid, she was finally, after over a year, able to share her story with her fellow group members. This not only gave her great relief—the group members just took in her story without judging her—but it enabled her to seek out the care she needed. Expressing her story began to make her whole again, and as that happened, her life changed.

An even more troubling story came from Suzanna. Her picture was a series of 29 square red marks of different sizes, covering the page. They represented the rapes and other abuses she had experienced. At the time she drew that picture, she was not able to tell a coherent story. She said quietly, "It was all the same," and shook her head. There were no good memories. The closest we could come to repeating her story was, "These were all the abusers; there are no good memories." Suzanna's picture, unlike the others, expressed an implicit memory, hidden and suppressed, without context or meaning other than being beaten down, violated, disregarded. It was likely that it would take her significantly longer to find herself—a self she could respect and live with.

There are, of course, joyful as well as tragic memory pictures—birthday parties, family outings, school successes—and these, like the heavier ones, gather a kind of gravitas, a meaning that may not have been recognized before. They help us put together the stories of our lives.

From these experiences of hearing stories and listening attentively, we learn something important as parents. We can transpose this listening experience to how we listen to our children. Do we, as parents, have the kind of time and self-control to just listen to our children? Can we join them in their emotions? Can we validate their feelings? Often, we do not. We are too busy with our daily responsibilities, and our children do not seem to have news that we consider important. Or we as parents feel we know better and are there to correct or enrich their experience before we even understand clearly what it is.

The art of listening to children isn't always an innate skill; it often needs to be developed. Listening means paying a certain kind of attention—attention to exact words and to the feelings behind the words. It means trying to understand it from a child's point of view. It is the art of being attuned to one's child, to acknowledge immediate information and to understand the implicit meanings behind that information. The attuned parent will understand what the child is feeling even if it is not directly expressed. A way of letting a child know he has been heard is to look at the drawing he brings home from school and to ask about it. It means repeating back the story he has just told you, then asking questions to learn more. The exercise here is just the first half, repeating what you have heard so that your child understands that you have attended to him, that he or she has been heard.

In some cultures, including some in the United States, there is the saying, "Children are to be seen but not heard!" I am making the assumption that this saying sustains itself because so many people do not know how to listen to and be interested in listening to their children. It has become a kind of self-serving mantra that justifies parents in disregarding their children. We, both adults and children, are more able to listen when we feel heard.

The stories we tell matter, and they give our children an essential sense of connection. The process of active, present storytelling is in itself healing and transformative as it implies empathy in the exchange of feelings and experience, often not overtly expressed. And it is through the sharing of stories that we discover that we could be everyone in all of them. As we share our stories, we define and redefine ourselves, learning from others and making sense of our lives rather than letting our history alone define us.

After experiencing a kind of emotional release at having been able to reconstruct a small piece of memory by drawing a picture of it and describing it to a group of participants, group members take another step back in time. Starting this deeper dive into the "forbidden past," parents encounter factual, and to some extent emotional, aspects of their lives they have barely visited, and then sometimes only by mistake. They make their way through a number of interventions, which they may experience as funny, painful, or both at once, which shed light on why they do what they do, how they feel about it, and what it's like to know yourself more deeply. This may come as a relief or possibly a burden—but in either case, it constitutes a hopeful way forward.

Early developmental trauma affects the body, feelings, relationships, trust, boundaries, one's sense of self, identity, thoughts, and self-worth. Fight, flight, or freeze are the common reactions to the "reawakening" of past, sometimes unconscious events, and these are the hallmarks of trauma. This is what we mean by being "triggered." These are normal responses to extreme distress. It is the body's way of responding to danger, and helps account for its survival.

But these strategies are often counterproductive in a non-stressful situation. There does not necessarily need to be an explicit recollection of the triggering event. Nevertheless, the "memory" has been implicitly recorded. What making meaning of traumatic history entails is creating a story from the disparate shards of experience, and being able to articulate it, to put it in its place in the past. Memory is unreliable, as Daniel Siegel suggests, but we have feelings about something which, if explored, can lead to a plausible story, which in turn gives some element of understanding to what otherwise can feel like a chaotic and unbalanced life. Getting to a life story that is coherent and makes sense to the holder of it is what the curative process is about. The individual becomes the "boss" of his or her own story.

Without this clarity, the traumatized person's "window of tolerance" can be quite narrow. The goal of therapeutic interventions is to help develop skills to widen the window of tolerance.

This process requires, in effect, moving back and forth from the present to the past—finding the antecedents which may be suppressed. Making the search in the presence of another trusted person or trusted group enables the process. The root of psychotherapy is based on this foundational truth, and in the work of a group, it can be amplified if the trusting base has been established.

In 1990, a research instrument was developed that attempted
to measure how we make sense of our lives. It was called the
Adult Attachment Scale (AAS). Daniel Siegel paraphrased some
of its questions: "What was your childhood like? How was your
relationship to your parents? To your siblings and friends? Who
were you closest to? Why? What memories do you have of your
childhood? Did you experience losses as a child, and if so, how
did you and your family react to them? Do you think your early
experiences impacted your adult life? Can you say how? How do
you think these early experiences affected your parenting?" This
was taking a deep dive into untapped memory.

Although the AAS was created after the beginnings of Parenting Journey, the similarities of these questions to those which Parenting Journey asks in its sessions are notable. They are aiming at
the same places of unrecovered memory. We were all searching for
ways to explain trauma and the effects of insecure attachments
in early childhood. Parenting Journey takes a circuitous route to
get to the answers, using humor, pictures, stories to get around
possible defenses.

An analysis of the AAS showed that, among the general population in the late 1990s, 40–55% of adults had insecure childhoods. Among the population which Parenting Journey serves,
the estimate is 80%.

All of these stories illustrate how different levels of trauma
have affected people's lives, often stalling them, making trusting
emotional engagement impossible, and instilling in the next generation similar fears, confusion, and blocks to safe, emotionally
rich lives.

Let us return to Colleen for a moment. Her life was restricted
largely to relationships with TV characters. Her children were

confused and frustrated by her lack of positive or warm emotion, her chaotic lifestyle, and her inability to care for them, or even to have any notion of what caring for children meant. She experienced the most severe level of attachment disorder, disorganized attachment. Disorganized attachment, as we discussed in chapter six, occurs when parents are very unattuned to their children, when they are frightening to their children, and when they themselves are also frightened. Unlike the other forms of insecure attachment, these children have not found strategies to deal with their impaired parents. They have run out of ways to cope.

What Colleen was warding off by the constant, 24-hour-a-day TV noise from different channels was the childhood story she could not make sense of—could not even remember clearly or explain. Eventually, after over a year of working with us, her story began to emerge. She had not been hiding it from me, as much as from herself. Small flickers of memory began to appear—life in a trailer park, messiness both in the park and in their trailer home. Her older brother seemed to have disappeared one day. She didn't remember why, and she didn't know what had happened to him. Nobody asked. She showed little affect in describing his disappearance, and apparently there was little affect on the part of her parents at the time of his disappearance. This continued to remain a mystery. What did begin to emerge was the story of a violent father who used to shoot not only animals but targets right around the trailer, developing a reputation as a dangerous and somewhat crazy person. He kept people at bay. The family was isolated, and she remembered, they rarely bathed. The family was ostracized, and Colleen was teased at school for arriving disheveled, dirty, and somewhat weird.

More exploration finally unearthed the biggest family secret. During Colleen's early teenage years, her father would send her mother out of the trailer, lock the door, and proceed to undress her slowly and seductively, and then rape her while whispering in her ear endearing sentences with promises he never kept. Her cries for help to her mother went unheeded. Her father would sometimes smother them with his hot, dirty hand. Her mother, standing outside, knowing what was going on, could not get in and was too scared to seek help. These events occurred with increasing frequency for several years. Colleen had nowhere to go, no recourse either at home or at school. She felt betrayed by both parents, and as she says, "Felt like garbage."

As an adult living with her own children, food and clothes, urine-soaked mattresses, and empty candy wrappers were mixed together in Colleen's apartment. The connections to the past were unmistakable. With the smell coming from her apartment as well as the family's shouting, neighbors called the DSS. This was how The Family Center and I had come to be involved in Colleen's life. As Colleen was reliving a part of her past, the housing authority was trying to evict her family. I asked them not to, to give me a little more time. They agreed. They gave *us* a month.

With that, I contacted the five neighbors who had filed the complaint, inviting them to come to a meeting with Colleen and me. They agreed, and after some discussion, we identified things that needed changing but also something that might be done to benefit the whole building wing. Colleen's children were cooped up all day long, except for Jimmy's participation in the soap opera, which was taking place at that time. I asked if there was something they might all participate in together, to bring Colleen and her kids out. Once the neighbors felt that someone was paying attention, they were all for helping find a solution.

It was summer. They agreed to buy a plastic swimming pool, collectively for the six families, and in this way, everyone would have an opportunity to get outside, to chat, to play in the water, and perhaps enjoy each other's company. Eventually, as Colleen watched her children having fun in the pool, she spoke to her neighbors and began to think of her life from a different perspective, to see that people were treating her respectfully, listening to her, sharing experiences that they all had been through, even laughing together. Little by little, she came to recognize and make some sense of her past. She could distinguish differences between her isolated and frightened life and a new one based on people who had no evil intention toward her.

The findings of Selma Fraiberg suggest that in cases where people are severely emotionally disabled, it is important to thoughtfully retrieve the feelings that traumatic events generated. These are often more difficult to reach than the events themselves (although sometimes it can be the reverse) and must be explored carefully at a rate that can be tolerated. It can entail years of therapy, and cannot be addressed by Parenting Journey in most cases—which is not to say that feelings do not come up. It is a next step for clients and for service providers to do this kind of in-depth work.

As Parenting Journey develops deeper partnerships with other organizations going forward, we hope this work will provide the kind of continuum needed to get to these deeper feelings. At this moment, there is no time to work through past traumas and to stay with our clients long enough to be sure they have found the feelings they need to address. The Parenting Journey program serves to open up tightly shut past experience, often manifested by tough and aggressive behaviors or substance abuse, or a kind of emotional frozenness. This is a first step toward working through what is necessary to meet and revisit Fraiberg's "ghosts in the nursery."

While Selma Fraiberg was focused on infant-parent relationships, she saw the parents' own traumatic experiences as interfering with their ability to see, feel, and understand the child's signals of need, and rather to see the child's behavior as that of the child being bad. What she noticed was an angry response and rejection by the parent of the child, caused by the "ghosts" of the parent's past—not the actual event, which may or may not be remembered accurately—but the repression of the affect associated with the terrible memories.

Parenting Journey in Burundi, a small African nation where we have taken the Parenting Journey program, has been named by its members "Opening Up." And that is exactly what it does. Through its many exercises and activities, interventions that bypass common defenses against facing the "ghosts" head-on, participants begin an opening up process toward elements of their suppressed past. And similar to Fraiberg's findings, this changes their lives and their behavior toward their children and spouses.

What is the common denominator of this approach that reaches across continents? Each exercise or intervention is based around a concrete physical or sensory element: visual, touch, sound, taste, hearing, movement, written words, dance, space, etc. Under safe circumstances, these exercises "open up" what is real right now and help "normalize" whatever a person is going through. Behaviors that may seem extreme are not necessarily "crazy." Individuals are often going through or have been through challenging, sometimes life-threatening situations, and something in the present moment is triggering a past experience. They may remember the event, or not. They may remember having these feelings but not the event.

More important is the underlying belief, conveyed through this process, that people are not born mean or ineffective, but rather they have experienced terrible things that have gotten in the way of the person and parent they want to be. The Parenting Journey process is one of trying in different nurturing and attentive ways to uncover the goodness, resilience, and strength in each person, and to have them begin to love themselves more.

One exercise, alluded to previously in chapter seven, is called the Mirror Exercise. It asks group members to look into a mirror and share what they see, what they like, what they do not like. The facilitator then asks what they were told as children about their appearance. After that, the facilitator asks what they are telling their own children about their appearance. This process introduces parents to the kinds of direct connections that exist without realizing it between at least three generations. Using the mirror has the effect of making it safer to disclose personal, embarrassing, or even painful elements of one's sense of self-worth and to assess how that gets communicated to the next generation.

In the example I described in chapter seven regarding a facilitator's attempt to get a group member to talk, the facilitator took the mirror, held it in front of herself, and said, "I see fat. I see ugly. I see skin that's too dark." Then she explained that this was the way she was taught to see herself and that, for years, she accepted it. Then she said, "But now I see my glowing black skin, my shining eyes, the beauty in the shape of my cheeks and lips."

When Tamika peered into the mirror, she said, "I see a strong mom, making my kids strong. But I'm also seeing what I need to change about myself. I'm looking at myself for my future goals. I got my strength from my mother, and I'm passing on her message to my kids: stay strong, be positive, be a proud black woman (to my daughters), a proud black man (to my sons). I tell them to love themselves and learn how to defend themselves. I tell them to know they will always be supported."

As part of the Mirror Exercise, the facilitator asked two more questions: "What do you think people think of you when they first meet you?" And "How would you like to be seen?" Tamika's answer to the first was, "They're a little intimidated, and they think I am funny and fun"; to the second, "I want to be seen as positive, survivor, strong, caring, reliable, supportive, determined."

Suzanna's reaction to being asked to look into the mirror was, "I can't do this. I was always the ugly one with the darkest skin. I don't want to look." Encouraged to try again, she quickly looked and then said, "I'm here because I need to know who I am. I always felt I shouldn't be in this world." Another try: "Suzanna, look into your eyes. What do you see?" "I see tears. I see fear. I see a kind person. Nobody ever told me I was pretty or worthwhile, except for my dad, my hero. But he disappeared. Nobody knows why, but I got the blame."

Suzanna's button read, "I'm brilliant, but I do dumb things." I raised this with her, reminding her of her button. What dumb things? She replied, "I hurt people. I hit my kids. I wanted to hurt my husband and my father. I wanted to kill my mother; I don't trust myself. I was abused as a child, forced to have sex with my mother's lovers. I was raped, used, thrown away like trash. I want to know who I am so I can be safe for my children and get them back from foster care."

This exercise regularly conjures up strong feelings. And that is its point. While not all answers to these questions are quite so deeply evocative, its game-like quality and the surprises it provides allow people to associate to feelings in an indirect way, thus getting beyond the protective shields of denial which characterize the ordinary encounters of their lives.

Another intervention, leading up to a more direct confrontation, involves asking people to grade their childhood. They are asked how they would rate their childhood on a scale of 1–10. They are asked about good memories from their childhood that they cherish, and about ways they were rewarded and punished. Then they are asked what their parents might have done differently that would have been better. These questions continue to raise awareness of people's own experiences, not necessarily traumatic ones, but they can create a starting point for how individuals can think more consciously about their own parenting styles. Most of us think that the way we were parented is the way it is, for better or worse. It is what we know, and as children, the only way we know. These exercises ask parents to step back and take a look, listen to others, and begin to feel some agency about their own lives.

The power of the group makes these exercises deep and effective. While people are describing events they remember, others are watching, listening, and remembering their own stories. They feel supported rather than blamed or freakish. They build on each other and realize theirs was not the only way to grow up.

Another way of reaching into the past asks group members to pick one of their parents, alive or dead, and to write them a letter, assuring them that this letter does not need to be sent. The letter can be anything that a person wants to say, or may have wanted to say for a long time, to this parent. It is an opportunity to open up, to say something the person never had the opportunity or the courage to say before. It can be a laudatory letter, thanking parents for all they did for their children, recognizing what the parents went through to accomplish this. It can show compassion, appreciation, and understanding. Or it can be a letter filled with resentment and rage. It can tell parents how they let down their children, and how much this individual has suffered from the behavior of her parents. Or it can be a mixture of the good and the painful. It is an opportunity to let out things that have simmered under the surface. Think how many times you have said something like, "If only I had said how much I loved and appreciated my mother. She always seemed to cut me off, but I should have pushed through. Now she is gone; it is too late."

Even though a parent is dead, the letter can have a cathartic effect. It *is* too late sometimes, but the act of articulating out loud, and reading it to others has a calming effect. It can be a metaphorical closure between adult child and parent. It can be a eulogy, or if the parent is alive, a kind of dry run for a letter or conversation that might actually take place. One woman in the group was assertively cussing out her father for his sexual impropriety with her as a child, and his continuing sexual baiting. Her letter was drawing a line. He could visit her and her children once a month, but he could not say the kinds of seductive things he was used to saying. Where she had been vague and distracted in the group until this moment, she now became crystal clear and focused. She then folded the letter up and said, "I think I'll pop this in the mailbox!"

When people read their letters to the group, they can ask for any kind of response they want. They can ask for applause, they can ask for silence, they can ask for personal reactions or questions, or for experiences others have had that remind them of the letter just read. The letter writing and readings allow for cathartic release, previously unexplored analysis, openings for change, often widening "the window of tolerance." Throughout the letter writing and sharing, there is a palpably powerful awareness and recognition of each individual's strengths and resilience.

Another intervention has to do with secrets and fears. It is approached in a humorous way, again to defuse defenses. People write on two small pieces of paper one secret and one fear that they have not shared with the group. They are told they will not be asked to share these secrets and fears. They are then instructed to fold the papers, placing one under one shoe, the second under the other. Then they're told to walk (or shuffle or slide) around the room, making sure to keep their secrets underfoot and unseen. This engenders laughter, movement, and physical connection to one another as people struggle with the task. The next step is to stand in a circle, tear up their secrets and fears, and throw them into the center of the room.

Everyone understands the metaphor. They discuss the meaning of this exercise to them, how secrets and fears inhibit their lives, and how much energy it takes to keep them hidden. The metaphor then continues with a ritual destruction of the papers, a ritual they decide on, either burning them, drowning them, flushing them down the toilet, etc. At this point, although they are not pressed to, participants often share their secret or fear.

For some people, this is the most emotionally fraught moment so far. Some share incest stories, rape stories, violent deaths—often for the first time in their lives. The window has widened; they are vulnerable, relieved, scared—a host of emotions, but they are never pushed to go farther than they want to go. A facilitator's caretaking and judgment are crucial in helping participants get what they need during the next period. If a trauma is revealed for the first time, we offer individual follow-up, or we refer the person to a therapist. No one leaves stranded.

Knowing that you are not alone is a great gift to others.

9

REWRITING NARRATIVES

Who Are You? Who Will You Be?

To be able to move ahead beyond the ghosts of the past and sense of deadlock, we face the obvious question: do we have a choice to do things differently? If we do not feel we have a choice, there is no point in trying to change anything. If there is no possibility of a different life or a different outcome, why roil the seas of discontent and make ourselves even more miserable?

The depression and sense of hopelessness we commonly see among our group members make this a very real and challenging problem. As leaders and facilitators, we have come to know and actually experience how trauma fractures attachments and often triggers a profound sense of powerlessness and disconnection. Many of our group members have never experienced a relationship they could count on, and therefore their stories are rife with constriction and limitations. The twelve-week Parenting Journey I program provides a challenging and nurturing process, enabling members to begin to move toward one another through sharing their stories. Each storyteller becomes critical to the process of connecting the past to the future and, in so doing, experiences the power of connection and belonging. Through this journey, a sense of aliveness, curiosity, and possibility emerges. What changes is *attitude*. Group members begin to make up new lives, guided by their fellow group members.

Rosamund Zander, in her book *Pathways to Possibility*, suggests that children's minds construct the world differently than the minds of mature adults. Faced with the inevitable traumas of childhood, children create the best narrative they are capable of, to explain those things they do not understand, cannot control, and that fill them with fear. In addition, when children have experienced "insecure attachment," many mildly adverse incidents, such as getting lost temporarily in the supermarket, are registered acutely. Children come up with narratives to explain what they can't comprehend; for instance, "I got lost because my mommy wanted to get rid of me. I have to be especially good." These narratives form beliefs as to how the world works, and stories about what to do in order to be safe and to survive. The stories tend to be "I"-centered, concrete, and hierarchical, and to deal in extremes (she w*ants* to lose me). When a story or a belief is sufficiently powerful to stick in a child's mind, the story itself may never develop further, even though the child continues to grow. These convictions about what's real stay put in the unconscious even in the face of compelling evidence to the contrary, and they manifest in our behavior. Thus, we continue seeing the world from the perspective of that helpless child: *"No matter what he says, I know my lover is planning to leave me."*

When we come to understand the phenomenon of "stuck narratives," we can rewrite them in a more adult form. We can say, for instance: "When I was a child, my mother was so erratic that the only story that made sense to me was that she was trying to leave me. Of course, that's not true because she could have found a way if she had really wanted to. She was just taking care of me in the same crazy way her mother took care of her. I realize I am very prone to interpreting any sign that my lover wants some distance in the context of the same childish story—that he is looking for a way to leave. It's probably wiser to take him at face value and attribute those thoughts to my 'story' rather than to him."

When we "rewrite" a story in this way and take on the new, more adult interpretation as reality, we are often flooded with compassion. We feel compassion for the lover who has been boxed in by our narrative, and the mother whom we see now as a suffering child herself, and for our own selves, who have undergone a lifetime of unremitting fear. And with each "child" story that we transform, we take a leap in growth ourselves.

The little girl who was always trying to please no matter what she was asked to do, even if it made her sad or uncomfortable, can, in her adult self, do what she wants, and say "no" with few, if any, repercussions. She develops a new "self," a new understanding about her place in a much wider world, and possibilities open up. Her attitude has changed with respect to what she sees and feels. She sees new possibilities. She is, in that sense, free.

Michael White was an early practitioner of narrative therapy. His approach is similar to Zander's and helps people to externalize their stories, and in so doing, participants can alter their stories and see them from a different perspective. This helps them move from hopelessness to possibility. Once the story is externalized, a person can develop.

A relatively recent form of therapy, known as Internal Family Systems, formulated by Dick Schwartz, explains a similar phenomenon somewhat differently. In his theory, consciousness is composed of three discrete parts or "constructs," subpersonalities, each of which is aimed at protecting us from some internal or external threats. These separate constructs communicate with each other, but not always harmoniously. Underneath these constructs and connecting them is the self, which incorporates characteristics such as lovingness, companionship, curiosity, calmness, creativity, cooperation. The self represents the spiritual center, our "soul," if you will.

The first of the three constructs is the manager. The manager controls the parts, attempting to make sure they perform their roles in a positive way. Its function is essential, but it can itself act in an overly rigid fashion.

Then there are the firefighters. These deal with crises, providing solutions that may be positive but sometimes are not. Firefighters may, for example, settle chaotic or panicky periods when current events overwhelm or past traumas rise up by protecting the psyche from shame or hurt through engaging in distracting, impulsive behaviors like drinking excessively, overeating, drug use, etc.

The third construct, exiles, represent traumas from the past—being lost, abused, isolated, disregarded in childhood. These traumatic memories—forcibly forgotten (exiled) experiences—are, for the most part, kept hidden by an overly rigid manager.

The goal of the therapy is to enable the individual to understand these parts and their functions, to connect and harmonize them, to negotiate their proper roles and bring them together under the healing and restorative aegis of the self.

What is the point of all this, and how does it affect Parenting Journey? While these notions have been around for many years, their most recent descriptions or interpretations (and the newly emerging schools of therapy) resonate with Parenting Journey in that they point to the solution to one's problems as lying within oneself and the ways one sees oneself. The facilitator helps clients to understand the different elements of their make-up and ask themselves whether these elements are collaborating in a useful way or not, and if not, what do they need to do to make it a beneficial collaboration? The facilitator provides hints along the way and techniques to help clients achieve a more fruitful introspection, but the real work is the client's own.

It takes significant effort to transform old childhood patterns into newer adult ones. The women in Tamika and Suzanna's group quickly bonded over their daily experiences, particularly the way they were treated and beaten down by the child welfare authorities. All had lost their children to some form of foster care at one time or another. These experiences triggered memories of their own helplessness as children in similar circumstances. Many had developed tough exteriors, tough language, and had engaged in dangerous encounters in the fast lane.

At the beginning of the group sessions, there was little personal ownership of the reasons for the behavior that had led to the participants' losing their children to DSS. This has the typical earmarks of a child fighting back as best he or she could, being angry, rebellious, and self-medicating in one way or another. While we were glad they bonded, bonding over the common experience of feeling wronged by the system was not all that helpful— even though their attitudes might have had merit, and one could sympathize with their feelings. But, in essence, they were looking outward for something external to fix their problems. They were not yet engaging with the myriad complexities within themselves. It was the frightened child finding other frightened children to "belong" to, and to fight the external enemy. Not that helpful, but it was a starting point.

Looking in the mirror, Tamika was the first to acknowledge that she was seeing herself with some approval, some disapproval, and looking for the person she wanted to become. Even Suzanna wanted to "find who she was" and to learn more about her seemingly unexplained violent outbursts. She still felt completely disempowered from achieving any sense of personhood. Yet she was in the room, and feeling like there *was* a person whom she needed to seek out and meet head-on. The work that groups do over the course of the program paves the way for hope through new awareness and change.

Having raised the notion that life is not static, and "reality"— what we perceive to be true—is heavily influenced by our childhood experiences, and at least to some extent can be moved around by the way we choose to look at it, we asked our group members to place themselves on an imaginary line, labeled from 1–10. One end of the line was represented by the phrase: "I believe that anything is possible if I just put my mind to it." The phrase at the other end of the line was, "I don't believe anything can change. My life is the way it is, and there's nothing I can do about it." The most positive pole was 10. The least positive was one.

Group members placed themselves in relation to these two phrases wherever they thought they fit best. Then we asked them to look at where they were in relation to the others, and asked them why they placed themselves where they did. The second question then was, "Are you surprised by where the others are standing? Do you want to ask them why they are there?"

Tamika placed herself at a nine in terms of her belief that change was possible. Suzanna was near the other end. There were lots of questions for Tamika. "How did you get there?" "What do I have to do to get where you are?" A concentrated discussion ensued where not only was Tamika providing answers, but the others were as well. They had begun thinking about themselves from a different perspective, forming creative alternatives to what they had assumed was "reality." Now, at least for some, they were ready to move on.

The first part of the next exercise raises the notion of complexity. Our lives are not one solid block of something, but rather, different elements operating inside our minds and emotions, as well as externally. People are asked to write down five things they like about their life and five things they do not like. Discerning and separating parts of one's experience are not something people always think about, especially when they are operating at extremes, either depressed or stressed, or extremely happy. Many people experience a kind of confusion and stasis—an inability to move—because they have not been able or willing to focus on the different elements of their lives.

Raising this complicated topic of different elements, even at a superficial level, introduces the notion that not all things are the same—everything bad or sad, or happy and perfect. Beginning to recognize differences is critical before even deciding that there is something to change.

The next part of the exercise asks that among the things they have chosen to want to change, participants pick one that is actually "changeable" (not "getting younger"). The group then assembles. With the lights dimmed, they participate in a guided meditation consisting of two parts. They have experienced relaxation meditations in the past, and this now is coupled with a so-called "miracle day" fantasy meditation, part of a solution-focused therapeutic intervention. They are asked to close their eyes and imagine they have fallen asleep in their safe place. While they are sleeping, a miracle occurs that will change their life. All the troubles and stumbling blocks they are facing disappear.

When participants awaken, they are asked, "What is the first thing you notice that lets you know that the miracle has happened? How does it feel to be free of the burdens? What do your children notice? What do your friends notice? Who is there with you? What are you doing? What kinds of conversations are you having? What does it feel like to be in this new place? What will you do on this first day after the miracle has occurred?"

When they have completed the fantasy, group members "return to the present" and share their "miracle" with the group. This is a profound experience for some people, who have long ago ceased to believe anything is possible other than what they currently have. Under normal circumstances, it's virtually impossible to imagine another life or another way of feeling about something, but this fantasy meditation encourages enough play to risk the unthinkable. If people can't let go of their stuckness, it's okay. This is just play.

An example might be imagining owning one's own home rather than renting shabby places or sleeping on other people's sofas. Another might be getting one's children back from foster care.

With their new image in mind, people fill out a chart and state what piece from their fantasy (or one of the five items they don't like and want to change, almost always a part of the miracle day fantasy)—they want to achieve. They mark down what their starting point for this change is—i.e., where they are now in relationship to the change. Then they fill out what it will look like if they arrive at their goal. This is a kind of cognitive behavioral therapy (CBT) exercise and helps people think concretely, rather than dream abstractly, and often obsessively, about how to get to the new place once they have envisioned it. From there, they are encouraged to think about the steps necessary to achieve their goal.

This is a critical part of the exercise because it is the one least understood or thought through. If the goal is owning one's own home, the first step might be getting a better-paying job, or going to school to become better educated for the type of work that a person might like and which would bring in income. (It is not winning the lottery.) Each one of these steps has several smaller steps within it, requiring focused attention. If the goal is getting one's children back from foster care, one of the first steps might be developing a good relationship with the foster care representative and seeking help in figuring out the most helpful steps. (There are usually service plans drawn up by the service providers, in collaboration with the client, which will help get the children back.)

Cleaning up one's apartment could be a step. The point is, these steps must be measurable, concrete, small, and doable. There may be many steps included in some of the more ambitious goals, such as getting a job. In terms of which items to pick to change, as long as they are possible and have motivation and passion behind them, any one will do, and can be a prototype for others. Many people say they want to do "more" or "less" of something, but this is insufficient. They need to specify how much of it will suffice to reach their goal.

Group members then collectively list the barriers to getting to their goals, and the resources they can call upon. These are noted on flip charts. In the course of two sessions, they have gone from fantasy to seriously focusing on something that is possible. Holding these two ends of a spectrum at the same time is challenging, and a valuable new skill.

We then come to "new habits," small ways where people can try out something new, test how it's going and see what it is accomplishing. A new habit might be as simple as setting the alarm clock 15 minutes earlier so that the morning rush is not so harried, and people are less likely to be late. Or a relational new habit might be to discuss with one's significant other or children something special about their day. Habits can take a significant period of time before they become part of a person's daily repertoire; persistence is required.

Rounding the bend of Parenting Journey I, we come to the anticipation of ending. Endings are critical, and very often painful. We look together at what makes a "good" ending and what makes a "bad" ending. Most of the members of our groups have experienced many more bad endings than good, and when they begin to dissect one from the other, certain truths come out, both at a generic level and a very personal one. People share their experiences of bad endings—violent deaths, the disappearance of a relative or a trusted service provider without notice, for example. And they discuss good endings—graduations, leaving home for a new life with a spouse, a good way to die, where all family members feel a sense of completion, to name a few. In some ways, this is a very heavy topic, and it coincides with the ending of our group. It allows the group members to create the kind of "good ending" they want for their group, and to practice what makes it good.

In line with a good ending is an exercise called "Appreciations," in which each group member writes a short note or word of appreciation to each group member. This provides each individual, often for the first time, with authentic expressions that he or she matters and has something positive and unique to offer. Receiving realistic and honest praise in writing forms an impression that may well conflict with one's self-image.

For the last 12 weeks we have been focusing on notions of self-image and how they actually stack up against "reality." Some people have come into the group full of self-righteous indignation, feeling they do not need to be here, and certainly not with "these people." This is often a cover for yet-to-be-discovered or acknowledged negative self-images, which in turn can manifest in bad behavior. Others enter with a sense of failure and futility. By the end of the 12-week process, each person has given a short assessment of what this other person has meant to her or him personally, and how the participant sees this person in the world. Appreciation notes are confirmations of strength and possibility, and show how differently one may be perceived from how one has been feeling inside. The hope is that this group acknowledgment of positive attributes will help facilitate the changes the group member hopes to make.

By now, the group has become a kind of family. The Appreciation exercise has two goals. One is to focus on another person—finding something special about each one. The other goal is to have people hear only "good news" about themselves.

Once the notes are written and read, first quietly to themselves, then aloud to the group, we make the connection to praising our children, and how important that is for their development. How do participants think their children would feel finding one of these messages in a lunch box or under a pillow, or simply expressed out loud?

Graduation is an extension of Appreciations and Good Endings. For many people in our groups, this is the first graduation they have ever participated in. They are asked to invite family members to attend, or service workers, or friends—anyone they wish. It is a joyful occasion, sometimes accompanied by large meals and dancing. The week before graduation, group members are given several questions to answer as they receive their diploma. For the last week, they can think of what they accomplished in the group, what goals they have set for themselves, what their next steps might be, and the resources they can call upon to help them. Lastly, they are asked what contributions they have made to the group, and they compare how they saw themselves coming into the program and how they experience themselves now.

The facilitator reads a letter to each member, affirming what he or she has seen in this person. The letter's intention is to confirm growth, to acknowledge challenges, some overcome, some not yet, and to encourage group members to continue the difficult journey they have agreed to embark on. For many people, this ritual and the receipt of this letter are some of the most affirming interventions they have ever received. They have felt nurtured, understood, challenged, and well taken care of, and they are now venturing out into the world with a consciousness of possibility that comes from a sense of their own agency to create their redefined and reimagined futures.

10

WE BECOME GLOBAL

Opening Up

TWIGURURE

By 2013, Parenting Journey had established itself with a great
deal of gratifying success in many venues in the United States.
Then, more or less by accident, we went global.

In late December 2013, I traveled with my 16-year-old grandson, Freddy, to a tiny hamlet called Kigutu in the mountains of
Burundi in East Africa. We were there at the invitation of my
friend Deogratias Niyizonkiza, an extraordinary man who had,
in 2008, inspired the people of Kigutu, his native village, to build
a health clinic with their own hands.

I had gotten to know Deo when we found ourselves sitting
next to each other at a small dinner party after the celebration
of the UN's 69th anniversary. We didn't know each other, but

bonded quickly. Pulitzer Prize–winning author Tracy Kidder had
written a book about him, *Strength in What Remains*, which followed Deo's life as a homeless refugee from the Burundian Civil
War, who made it to New York. He taught himself English while
surviving by delivering groceries. He later miraculously found
his way to Columbia University and Dartmouth Medical School.

The war Deo fled from was Burundi's version of the Rwandan
genocide, an interethnic conflict between the country's Tutsi and
Hutu populations that led to one human tragedy and atrocity
after another—including widespread massacres, the devastation
of farming and food supplies, and the use of child soldiers on
both sides. The 12 years of war broke the country, which had
already been one of the very poorest on earth. The war more or
less ended in 2005, 8 years before Freddy and I visited, but people
were still starving and dying for lack of basic medical care. One
out of seven women died in childbirth, and child mortality was
staggeringly high.

Deo's vision was, first of all, to provide Kigutu with health
care and basic education about such things as nutrition, safe sex
practices, schooling, preventive health measures, and other primary needs. But additionally, he believed that by collaborating on
common interests, the Tutsi and Hutu people in the community
would no longer be motivated by hatred and violence toward
each other. They weren't actually killing each other any longer,
but the fear, anger, and vengefulness hadn't disappeared either.

Deo wanted to do something to change this. To bring his
plans to life, he inspired Kigutu's people to build a clinic with
their own hands. The idea worked. Women fired the bricks and
placed them one upon the other until the rudiments of a clinic
came into existence. The next project was bringing water over

two mountains from fresh springs and storing it in tanks, and then, once this had been accomplished, bringing electricity via solar panels to a place that had never had electricity.

This was the vision of a man who grew up in these mountains and was determined to bring his homeland back to life. Deo inspired the people to think differently about their lives. He showed them that with hard work and the will to succeed, their lives could improve. He brought in doctors and nurses. Deo himself had been a doctor-in-training in Burundi before the war, and now he had returned from the United States with an MPH (Master of Public Health). He knew what was necessary. Deo traveled the world, bringing in volunteer experts to teach local people things like farming techniques, how to build co-ops, what is healthy food and what isn't, how to manage finances, and how to read. Preschool and after-school programs were added to the very poor state-run local elementary school. Children had drumming classes where they learned traditional instruments and dances, a part of the culture the war had all but destroyed.

In Kigutu there was barely enough to eat (often only one meal a day of rice and beans, and sometimes not even that). People lived in shacks with leaky tin slabs for roofs, dirt floors, and no plumbing. But Deo's energy and will to change things were contagious. Even with hunger, illness, early death, and grinding poverty, a new spirit of joy and optimism emanated across the area. In addition to the clinic, Kigutu's people built a community center where children came to dance, and adults came for meetings. More and more, people in the community resonated to something positive happening, and they joined in.

The next big project was to build a real hospital, to be called the Women's Health Pavilion. Its primary goal was going to be to provide safe births, caesarian sections when necessary, and to otherwise save lives. Volunteers in the community showed up with their hoes and began preparing the land where the hospital would be built. They sang as they worked. Deo had a kind of fetish about flowers and beauty, so by the time I arrived, even on my first visit 2 years into the project, the paths and beds were flourishing with cosmos and other flowers, many of which were originally slips Deo had "liberated" from restaurants and hotels.

My second visit, with Freddy, came at a time when Deo had decided it would be important to add a mental health component to the village's services. He explained to me that 12 years of violence had produced a high level of post-traumatic stress among the villagers, and that even with all the new energy and spirit, depression was endemic. Freddy, my grandson, and I spent Christmas on a plane in order to reach Kigutu by December 27, when an annual community forum was to take place. Freddy's task was to bring 20 app-loaded iPads to the children and to teach them how to use them. My task was to start a community mental health program.

I told Deo that I didn't know the Burundian culture at all. I had been to Kigutu one time before, but the visit had been fairly brief, and the language barrier kept me from talking to more than a very few people (the community members speak only Kirundi). Consequently, I told him I felt I had very little to contribute.

But Deo was persistent, and eventually, I said to myself, "Have confidence. Deo believes you can do it. Maybe you *can* do it." I decided to get involved. I remembered how I had approached working with people from the housing projects when the Family Center first started. That, too, was a culture I didn't know. As a result, I had come into the experience acknowledging that I did not know very much about the people I was going to be working with, and that I needed to learn from them. That had been effective. It had helped build trust, had opened the way for real conversation, and had helped us find truly useful ways of being of service. I was Columbo back then, and a little of Dorothy too, knowing nothing, but curious to learn. In Kigutu, I could be Columbo again. I would learn from the people in Kigutu. I would listen carefully, and something would happen.

Deo introduced me at the community meeting, but as he spoke in Kirundi, I had little idea what he said about me. Then it was my turn to speak to a room of 400 people. I told them what I did back home at Parenting Journey. I told them that I wanted to hear from them so I could learn what they saw to be their most pressing problems, aside from poverty and ill health. I asked them to teach me so that perhaps we could find common ground where we could try to solve some problems together.

I was concerned that they might not speak up, and I had prepared a few games to try if that was the case. But speaking up turned out not to be a problem. Many of them spoke up, for about an hour. The women said, even in the presence of their husbands, that the most important thing to them was for their husbands to "stop beating them." I marveled at their bravery.

The men spoke up too. They said they "didn't know how to have a conversation," or at least that was how the translation came across. What they meant was that they didn't discuss things with their wives or children. They kept things to themselves. The idea of a family conversation was simply foreign, unheard of. A helping professional might say they were "closed off." Part of it, I learned later, was cultural. Men weren't in the habit of revealing feelings or entering into discussions with women or children.

Also, the terrible killing that had gone on during the war wasn't a matter for discussion. Many had suffered, and many had caused suffering. Things were better left unsaid, which contributed to the culture of constriction and silence.

The men did speak at the meeting, though. No one reacted to the wives' assertions about domestic violence, but they did say they weren't used to talking, that they didn't know how. I thought that was something I'd want to explore later.

Even though three days before New Year's Eve was a busy time in this community, preparing feasts and celebrations, I asked if there were a few people who might meet with me the next day to educate me a bit more. Five women raised their hands. This was perfect. Deo agreed to translate for me, and I asked each one to bring an object that mattered to them. The next morning, I walked into the community center, and there were 90 women there, not five—each one with an object. My thoughts of a small, intimate gathering had gone out the window, and for a few moments, I was at a loss.

Then I remembered I had been doing something for many years that might work with this large group. I asked them to break up into groups of nine or 10 and to introduce themselves to each other and tell a story about their name, and then tell the group about the significance of the object they had brought. Two hours passed, and they were not ready to leave; they were still talking. Parenting Journey's first two activities had won the hearts of these women and were more powerful than I could have imagined.

Names in Burundi, unlike most names in America, have great significance and tend to refer to important family events. Sometimes these events are not happy, as in "my name means 'nobody likes me'" or "I am the fifth child, my four older siblings are dead." Other names praise God, as in "Deogratias" or other versions of praising God's mercy. In one of the small groups which I attended, every woman had brought a hoe. They explained that this represented their power in the family as they were the gardeners who grew the crops and fed the family.

From this first meeting, a partnership developed between the women, some men, and myself, a partnership built on hope and the belief in the possibility of a better life. They had a spirit that said, "We can do it; we can change things for the better." While it seemed that I had brought to this gathering a framework for a possible community mental health program, I suggested we all learn together. The greatest reward for me was that they were willing to speak up and to challenge me (though not in the beginning) and to start fashioning a program that they could own.

It struck me that I was seeing here in this rural Burundian village the same spirit of hopefulness and possibility that characterized Parenting Journey groups elsewhere. They believed something could be different and were willing to give it a try. As we developed the program over the next 18 months, using concrete, tangible exercises, we saw villagers begin to talk to their children and to play games with them—which was, for the most part, not their usual custom. Couples started discussing issues that never were discussed before, like the use of money, how to raise their children, the importance of sending their children to school, as well as their relationships to each other. Previously, it was the men who had made all these decisions. Now the women were finding their voices, and they were being listened to. It took immense courage on the part of both the women and men to try on a way of relating that was so different from what they were used to.

After several more visits to Burundi, I thought it was time for the community leaders whom I had been training to develop and run this program to give it a name. We took a large piece of paper, pinning it up on the wall. I asked them to call out some names. A long list developed. I had no idea what it said—it was all in Kirundi. But I asked them to vote on their favorites. The winner was *Twigurure*, roughly translated, "Opening Up." Although I could not pronounce it, I felt it was the perfect name. Opening up is what frees people from hidden trauma, from fear, from isolation, from having to fight. It opens conversations, seeking new pathways to creativity, happiness, joy, appreciation, and risk-taking. It assumes that people can change. I have named this book "Opening Up" in honor of the courage of these people and the hope for the future that the phrase carries.

Parenting Journey has now been operating in Burundi for 7-plus years. At the end of each weekly session, there is a closing ritual chosen by a member of the group. Sometimes it's a meaningful gesture on everyone's part, but usually it is a song. At their graduation ceremony—after completing 17 sessions, which adds a few to our American curriculum—families and friends come to celebrate. People dance and sing. Musicians play. Everyone eats rice and beans and drinks Fanta. A graduation can take all day!

What these people have been able to achieve is a change in attitude from anger, fear, and depression to one of hope and belief that what was once impossible in family and neighborly relations is possible. While this is not yet universally the case in the community at large, and there is a long struggle ahead to involve greater numbers in this new way of thinking and being, they have the beginnings of a transformation, not only in attitude but in terms of concrete action. Flattened stares and suppressed anger have changed to smiling, expressive faces and the release of good energy that has long been bottled up.

As of 2020, about 1,000 people have gone through the program, and there are about 20 leaders running groups. We have added a second group curriculum, which focuses on good ways to have conversations, and provides nonviolent responses to conflict. "Opening Up" has also precipitated a women's movement. Women who have graduated from Twigurure are spreading the messages they have learned, or taught themselves, from the small knoll of Kigutu to other villages. They are speaking up about how to connect with women throughout the country to build their voices, which have hitherto been silent.

COUPLES

At our initial meeting, now 7 years ago, women almost universally spoke of domestic violence being their first priority. That had amazed me since their husbands were sitting right there in the crowd. The wives pressed me to address this as part of the curriculum, but I could not think of a safe way to do it. It was obviously too volatile a subject, with cultural roots that I might not have understood sufficiently well, and the last thing I wanted to do was precipitate even more aggression. Our second Twigurure program focused on what the men had identified as their biggest problem—difficulty in having a conversation. Our sessions on that were going well, but how could we deal with domestic violence without shaming the men into greater anger and worse consequences?

Then I had an idea. One day I asked Deo to collect 25 of the most violence-prone men in the community and 25 women, including the 12 individuals I was then training as leaders for the Twigurure programs. I spoke to each group separately, saying to them: "Have a conversation amongst yourselves and come up with four or five things you want to tell the other gender. Then come up with four or five questions you have for them. Nominate two in your group to be speakers for your collective thoughts. We'll all meet in two hours."

The men and women had been revving themselves up for this. Substantial changes had taken place among many of the villagers in the time we had been operating in Kigutu, but the crucial frustrations of wives and husbands with each other were still ongoing, and now we were focusing on those emotions. There was lots of barely suppressed hostility in the air. The groups came together and had a brief encounter—two from each side. I still don't know what they said as I didn't want to interrupt the flow with translation, but the tense, angry body language told me a lot of what I needed to know.

Ten minutes in, I asked them to stop and reassemble themselves, this time in groups of 12 with equal numbers of men and women, and to continue the conversation. I facilitated one of these groups.

At first, members in each group were hurling insults at each other, but gradually the tone changed. From "The women never work; they don't make money," to "Well, actually women always have a baby on their back, a hoe in their hand; they tend the garden and make the family meals." You could hear the men softening up. Women, too, went from blaming men for spending all their money on beer, to acknowledging that some of them did their best to bring in money and that sometimes the men were helpful with buying things for the family.

Trying to encompass everything they were saying, I constructed a narrative and repeated it back to them. It was something like: "It sounds like men leave in the morning; women get the children dressed, ready for school, take them to school, then work in the garden and make dinner for the family. The father often doesn't come home to eat but returns later, drunk. The wife is angry and doesn't speak to him. He is angry that she won't speak, and he doesn't speak either. He goes on drinking until, later on, they begin a physical fight. Is that right?" They all nodded their heads. That's what seemed to be a common pattern.

I then said, "So what do you want to do about it?" At first there was silence. I imagined they were expecting me to have an answer. Then one man hesitantly raised his hand and said, "Maybe we could remember back to when we were courting our wives when we were in love. We could remember how that was and try to start over." Another man said, "Maybe we could ask each other, how was your day?" I teared up. I told them these were wonderful ideas and that in Twigurure we have an exercise called "new habits." These two are perfect examples of new habits, and scientists have proven that if you practice a new habit for 28 days, it can become a part of your life. I suggested they might try it.

Three months later, I returned, and we did the same exercise. There were many couples at the meeting. I told them they could join the same small group as their spouse or a different one. My group had four couples, including the man who had made the first suggestion at our last meeting. I recognized him and asked him if he had practiced his new habit. Beaming, along with his wife, he described how every Saturday morning, they take a walk in the hills, holding hands and talking—like they did when they were courting. Then another woman, looking somewhat embarrassed,

jumped up and threw her arms around her husband's neck, saying, "This is what we do!"

This was a domestic violence intervention without ever men-
tioning those shaming words. It differs in many respects from
what we do in America. In the United States, it's deemed safe
only to keep the genders separate. In the Twigurure programs in
Burundi, we now begin by separating the genders, but then we
put them together to problem solve as a group. There may initially be anger and attacks—though not spouse on spouse—but
those give way. The structure demands that members come up
with solutions, not get the answers from "experts." It becomes
a community conversation, an intervention which is safe and
which builds upon a group effort to find positive solutions. By
not having actual spouses together in the first phase, the "spousal
argument" can take place without actual harm. Then the members of this "gender conversation" can return home and practice
what they have learned from the larger group.

MIL MILAGROS

In the spring of 2016, Parenting Journey was invited by Mil
Milagros ("A Thousand Miracles") to bring our program to
Guatemala. Mil Milagros is a program that feeds stunted, malnourished children in eight schools in the northwest, indigenous
area of the country. It was founded in 2007 by Margaret Blood,
whom I had known for years through her work with children in
Massachusetts.

In the region where Mil Milagros operates, almost
three-quarters of the children are chronically malnourished. The
education level is the lowest in Latin America. Many people are

illiterate, and there are 22 indigenous dialects spoken. The population, much as in Burundi, is impoverished. Also, like Burundi, Guatemala suffered through many years of a murderous civil war that reached near-genocidal proportions, with the indigenous population bearing the brunt of the violence.

Mil Milagros is organized around boards of mothers and grandmothers who work to improve schools, further basic hygiene efforts, and, most importantly, improve childhood nutrition by preparing healthy meals for schoolchildren in their communities. But as the Mil Milagros project progressed, Margaret Blood realized that in addition to providing food and teaching mothers how to cook healthy meals, the organization could train the mothers and grandmothers in their programs to become community leaders on a broader scale. The women who had been part of Mil Milagros were smart, competent, and motivated; they had potential to broaden Mil Milagros's impact.

Dr. Barry Zuckerman, a friend and colleague of Margaret Blood, is also on the Parenting Journey board. "It's all about the moms," he told Margaret. "If you want to move forward, you have to build their capacity to support one another." With a track record of success in Burundi with similar demographics, Parenting Journey seemed like a perfect fit to help do this. When Margaret approached me, we spent hours together strategizing how to do this most effectively, then three of us from Parenting Journey visited Guatemala to see the problems and Mil Milagros's approach firsthand.

Together we trained Margaret's staff, along with 10 Mil Milagros mothers, in the Parenting Journey model. This training proved to have benefits beyond Margaret's expectations, as it became a vehicle for the staff to cohere and improve

communication and teamwork from their differing locations. At
every staff meeting they use the ritual questions, and focus on the
importance of self-care amidst daunting challenges of poverty
and geography.

Now in its fourth year, Parenting Journey at Mil Milagros has
formed partnerships with mayors in the various towns where they
work, and some municipal staff are being trained in Parenting
Journey to further build momentum for women to use their skills
and their voices. Margaret claims that the name "Parenting Journey" might be a misnomer, because the core program is applicable
well beyond parenting. It helps women build effective organizations and, in the case of Mil Milagros, as well as Burundi, healthy
communities.

Now, in both Burundi and Guatemala, a world away from each
other, women and men's voices are joining and working together
to build a new community. They are challenging the traditions
of male-dominated privilege and improving the likelihood that
there will be less family violence, more attention to education
(especially for girls), and better health for all.

11

THE FUTURE

Continuing the Journey

Everyone is involved in parenting. We would not be here on this planet if we were not. We all came from a mother and a father. And almost always, there is someone who takes care of us as children—biological parents, adoptive parents, foster parents, grandparents, older siblings, childcare workers, friends, neighbors, relatives—even if it is just one person parenting alone. A great many of us are also parents ourselves, and therefore know parenting from at least two perspectives, although within those two perspectives, there are hundreds if not thousands of permutations.

Parenting is a journey. We start at birth and end at death. Whether child or parent, with every growth moment, large or small, we are readjusting our choices, our needs, our abilities,

our usefulness, our desires. Some developmental changes are well
known and anticipated, but some come with peculiar caveats, and
some with unanticipated and unknown elements. We take care of
the young, who in turn end up the caretakers of the aging. Our
lives could be sailing along smoothly when a growth moment or
a tragedy derails either or both parent and child. There is no such
thing as stasis. We are always moving, always journeying. And
with this movement comes the unknown and learning. Who do
we learn from how to tackle the next step?

In this book we have discussed a few ways of raising children, some that have been shown to work, and others that are
shown not to work. And by "work," I mean raising a healthy,
well-adjusted, thoughtful, generous person with the capacity
to love, to feel empathy, to have friends, to be happy, to work at
something, and to contribute to the general good. Some of us, as
parents, feel that our lives are succeeding in a positive way and
that we are raising children to also live full lives. Others of us are
stuck someplace and feel unsatisfied with our lives. We may not
feel safe; we may not have enough money or stable or fulfilling
work. We also might not have good friends or healthy children or
happy intimate relationships. We may feel the destructive effects
of racism in our daily lives.

Our Parenting Journey programs may have helped reduce,
and even in certain situations, eliminate some of these difficulties,
but we do not know for sure how deeply, or for how long. As an
evidence-based program, we know the effects of our programs
to some degree, yet we can never be exactly sure how our interventions play lasting parts in clients' lives. Sometimes a small
gesture—like a gift of makeup, help painting a living room wall,
or lunch together—for a pained soul can become a turning point

in that person's life. Sometimes all the expertise of a knowledge-able clinician or specialized program that seems just right has no impact. It is hard to predict. It is even harder to evaluate using conventional metrics.

Metrics are valuable and useful to get us partway there, but beware of the cost of counting too much on academic "instruments" that claim to measure well-being. We humans are way more complicated than these metrics, and most of us don't live our lives in easily measurable ways. There are many programs and interventions out there that can be more easily measured. A school program, for example, can measure how many children succeeded in graduating to the next class or made it through college. Well-being doesn't have the same kinds of clear steps. Becoming sober or obtaining employment are measurable things, but they do not tell the whole story of a family or a life!

Our track record at Parenting Journey shows that our pro-grams can have an impact on the work of organizations outside our own, such as schools, community centers, and agencies. In the 30-plus years that we have been operating, in addition to running our own parent groups, we have expanded to roughly 500 sites—by training people from other agencies, schools, and communities in the Parenting Journey model. In this book, I have concentrated on describing the trajectory of one program (of six iterations) from its roots in housing projects to an internationally replicable model. Our next phase will include using the knowledge we have gained from practice, new information on the effects of stress and trauma on individuals, and from staff and families themselves. Our inten-tion is to go deep and broad, to spread Parenting Journey all over the world. We will become principally a training program.

Humanity is now facing existential challenges that are bigger than all of us and that are affecting all of us. The world is changing. Familiar categories of identity are breaking down and becoming something else. Globalization, immigration, the displacement of refugees, and the joining of our cultures through marriages and friendships are colluding with the internet and social media to bring together people from all over the world, many of whom are not used to being together. We are becoming increasingly aware of the lasting effects of racism in our own country.

Climate change, too, is bringing us together in often new and frightening ways. As our habitats change, our cultural traditions and histories, which are often tied to the land, and the identities that go with them, are as much in danger of being displaced (or in some cases, erased) as we are. The land that we have lived on for thousands of years, or even just 50 years, may, in the future, no longer accommodate our rituals and ways of life. For some, these changes are already taking place.

Such change and differentness are frightening to many who may be feeling their identity sliding away, and may feel that they are being pulled into a new reality by these global changes and by neighbors who look different, speak different languages, pray differently, and behave differently. What we don't know, we tend to be afraid of and to see as possibly hostile. This has been the case throughout human history. The difference now is that as the world gets "smaller" through mega-communication at multilevels, the need to manage "difference" is more intense.

While politicians will tackle the challenges of developing countries, ordinary people are increasingly challenged to figure out where they belong. Their first inclination will be to focus on the parts of their identity that they feel they are being forced to give up, be it race, ethnicity, religion, tribal or social habits, culture, political views, gender roles, and others. Those who have belonged to groups that have traditionally occupied positions of power are feeling these changes particularly strongly—whiteness, patriarchy, heterosexual marriage practices, to name a few. But as this rupture of the known world order happens, other structures will develop.

Within the frame of this changing world, our work at Parenting Journey may take on a different relevance. On a very small scale so far, we already have a paradigm that works in other countries and faraway places like Burundi and Guatemala. While there are programmatic adjustments that are needed to fit a particular culture, we have experienced a hunger on the part of these partnerships to expand their knowledge and sense of new possibilities. When I first went to Burundi and listened to women there speaking about the extent of gender bias, I told them the story of the women's rights movement in the United States that started 50 years ago. They were astonished. Ever since our first Parenting Journey meeting in Burundi on the International Day of the Woman, these women have gathered regularly to plan how to spread the words and experiences they have encountered through Parenting Journey throughout their district, and eventually, throughout their country. What they are spreading is the value of respecting one another, of striving to eliminate ubiquitous domestic violence, of learning how to have good conversations with spouses and with children, of respecting and inviting the views of children, of playing with children, and of valuing themselves. This does not seem very different from what we in America value and strive for, or what other people around the globe strive for.

What we have learned in Burundi can be applied to people all over the world. Now is the time for us to stand up and take a leadership role in finding the means to access what we know can affect people over the world. We know our programs work. There is no reason not to try. And there is every reason to bring people together in healthy ways rather than in fearful and dangerous ones.

Instead of counting on familiarity of culture or skin color, we will focus on the art of relationship building and better personal self-understanding. Through the Parenting Journey programs, people can learn how to have difficult conversations. When one can clearly speak one's feelings and thoughts without fear, one need not take out the sword. The first rule of a good conversation is the notion of respect for the other, no matter how different they may be. The second rule is curiosity.

"Everyone," said Harry Stack Sullivan, a famous psychiatrist, "is more simply human than otherwise, and more like everyone else than different." The Parenting Journey's aim is to be useful. If our work has been to any degree successful, it is because it emanates from the recognition of a shared humanity with our clients. Out of such awareness, human services institutions are born. One wants to help others not only out of a sense of compassion and duty, but also because we better understand who we are, and our lives are enhanced by doing so. By allowing us into their lives, the clients of Parenting Journey have taught us how to better support them. But it isn't only the families who gain from these relationships; the workers who serve them are rescued too. Working together, we all try to free the human spirit to be its best possible self. We change our attitudes and beliefs in ourselves to be more than we ever thought we could be. Everyone needs everyone.

If the Parenting Journey has been achieving the work it aspires to do, it is not because a particular intervention worked. Underneath these interventions lie motive and purpose that are larger and more encompassing. The Parenting Journey is everyone's journey. The loneliness addressed is everyone's loneliness. The suffering is everyone's suffering. Together, every day, we learn how remarkable it is to be simply human.

Appendix

THIS APPENDIX GIVES A BRIEF DISCUSSION OF THE FACILITA-
tor training programs and Parenting Journey's evaluation as an
evidence-based organization.

FACILITATOR TRAINING

The way we decided to expand our reach beyond what our own
staff could do was to create a five-day facilitator training program for each of our curricula. These are in-depth, experiential,
"from the inside out" learning experiences, taught by experienced
facilitators, who take trainees through all 12 or 14 sessions of
a program in three days and then spend two days reflecting on
group facilitator skills, practice sessions, and the nuts and bolts
of getting a group started. There are detailed guides for each of
these six curricula, and a training academy where, at least once
a year, trainers gather from across the country for further discussion and learning about what must change in a curriculum and/
or how it must be taught.

The training model follows the same format for all groups.
Over 2,000 people have been trained as facilitators, and they
are operating in over 500 locations, many in the New York area.
As an example, I will describe parts of a training session for

facilitators learning how to run the men's groups. The following excerpts from a report from one of our facilitator trainers, Amy Brinn, provide examples of how a five-day training for the men's group curriculum was delivered and received by mostly male facilitators.

Day 1:

The training group consisted of 12 men, and it was facilitated by one man, Shawn, and myself. They are mostly Black and Latino. They all work with disenfranchised families and are deeply committed to supporting them, with a special interest in reaching out to fathers. They are all working in the trenches with devotion and love. Two are pastors. They range in age from early twenties to 60+, from parent advocates to seasoned clinicians and community organizers.

They resonated with the film clip from *The Pursuit of Happyness*, and the themes, assumptions, and research we presented about fathering. Everyone rocked to the music of Michael Jackson's "Man in the Mirror." The "Man in the Mirror" session went deep, exploring ideas and messages about manhood they received growing up and what they want to model for their sons and daughters. They were already engaged about the roles of their fathers and mothers and how it has affected them.

Day 2:

We started with a warm-up exercise: "If you could have lunch with any man, alive or dead, fictional or not, who would it be and why?" The answers were: Bob Marley, Richard Pryor, a heroic bystander who rescued a child from a shark, Richard Wright, Geronimo, LBJ, MLK, Barack Obama, Jay Z, Al Bundy. Shawn facilitated the connecting themes. Then we had a line sculpture where people placed themselves on an imaginary line with respect to these two statements: "I am my father" and "I am not my father," wherever they felt the statement best resonated with them. They talked about why they were in this place on the line and asked others what had put them in different spots.

They had been asked to bring a special object, something connecting them to their father or an important man in their current life. Some examples were: A Masonic ring, a tattoo of their child's name, a photo of Muhammad Ali shouting, "What is my name?", a picture of the last Xmas morning before his parents got divorced, a picture of King Tut, a photo of a light fixture his father had installed.

Throughout, the exercises went deep; their empathy toward each other was intense, with lots of belly laughs, storytelling, affectionate ribbing and bro love—probably pent-up with little normal, acceptable outlets. One of the most heartbreaking exercises is a letter which they write to their father, probably the heaviest moment in the training.

Day 3:
Started with a clip from *Fences* and a line sculpture about their belief in the possibility of change. Then they participated in a collage exercise, similar to PJII but more intense, using photos and pictures, creating visions of what they might want to have in their lives. We had music in the room. There was lots of shouting out: "I need a spiritual picture, bro!" "Are you finding yourself a partner?" "Man, I've found three."

The aspirational aspect came through, and participants related to each other's work. In another session, they answered questions pertaining to the family they grew up in and the family they live in now. They then did a gallery stroll of the collages, with two questions: "What jumped out at you from other people's collages?" and "What aspects of fathering would you like to work on, which might serve as a goal for the next session?"

These excerpts give an idea of what the first three days of a facilitator training might look and feel like, coupled with the theoretical underpinning for each exercise. What is missing from this description is the depth of theoretical understanding needed to effectively use the various experiential options as well as training in group process. As we become more of a Training Institute these elements will be expanded. Add to that another two days of practice in group process, different role-playing exercises, the nuts and bolts of getting a group off the ground, as well as gaining a familiarity with the curriculum—and trainees are ready to get started, always working in pairs for at least the first three groups. After finishing the training, they stay connected to us and can receive technical assistance as needed. The training experience is enriching for its learning content, but even more for the participants' personal and professional growth.

When some graduates from different trainings were asked some months later how this experience affected them personally, professionally, and whether it had an effect on their agency, they gave inspiring accounts of personal growth and insights, and several said that in addition to learning how to run a Parenting Journey group, they had changed their way of seeing families. What this meant was that as, for example, child protective workers, they had often seen parents as the adversaries of children's best interests. Now they had come to see that parents' life experiences had affected how they were able to parent their children, how they themselves wanted to change. Parents wanted to be the allies of child welfare workers, as well as of children. In two striking instances, people reported that as a result of several staff having been trained in Parenting Journey, even before running a program, the philosophy of the agency itself had been affected as to how to approach and relate to its clients.

EVALUATION

Ours is an evidence-based preventive program and strategy. Measured against diagnostic therapies, out-of-home placements, institutional costs, incarceration, and loss of revenue, increasing the costs of a more robust and effective preventive approach would be minuscule. In fiscal year 2010, of the $13.6 billion in federal funds spent on child welfare, the Title IV-E funds (monies for children being removed from their homes in the form of foster care, adoption, and independent living) comprised over half the allotment, whereas the Title IV-B funds to states (funds dedicated to keeping families together, preventive interventions) comprised just under 5%. We must move toward reversing these numbers.

As an organization, Parenting Journey has been evaluated over a 7-year period by the Institute for Community Health, an independent affiliate of Harvard University, and also has achieved evidence-based recognition in a randomized controlled study in partnership with ABCD Head Start in Boston, Massachusetts, using a quasi-experimental study design. All study participants completed the Parenting Journey Survey and the Parenting Stress Index at the beginning of the study (the baseline) and again at follow-up. Two hundred and forty-four parents were in the study; 123 in the Parenting Journey group and 121 in the control group. Of the 244 participants, 52% were born in the United States,

48% born outside the United States, 31% were African American, 39% Hispanic/Latino, 17% White, 3% Asian, 10% other or mixed race. Approximately 70% of participating families live on a household income of less than $24,600 per year. We evaluated this group-based curriculum on improving parental strengths in key areas known to promote family well-being and to protect against poor outcomes for both parents and children. They were: hope and optimism, insight on upbringing and present parenting behavior, identifying personal goals, self-efficacy, ability to nurture self, self-awareness, and social networks. Of the seven constructs, three were adapted from existing measures, and four were developed specifically for the Parenting Journey evaluation.

In addition, we used the Parenting Stress Index to assess three subscales: parental distress, parent-child dysfunctional interaction, and difficult child. These three taken together yield a total parental stress score. Intervention participants were significantly more likely to demonstrate improvement in four or more of the seven constructs measured by the Parenting Journey Survey. For two of the seven constructs, specifically, "Insight on Upbringing and Its Effect on Parenting Behavior" and "Ability to Utilize Social Networks," intervention participants demonstrated statistically significant improvement on scores from baseline to follow-up versus comparison group participants. On the Parenting Stress Index, intervention participants' mean total stress score decreased by 14.1 points, while comparison participants increased by 3.0 points. Among a low-income, diverse parent population, participation in Parenting Journey is associated with improvement in reported strengths and decreased stress.

A story about Parenting Journey in schools leads us to believe that more purposeful involvement in schools is an important way to proceed. In Brooklyn, New York, PS 503, Parenting Journey was run several times, and the principal reported the following:

> We have had so much success with the Parenting Journey. Based on feedback from participants, parents have instituted structures for their families—like nightly dinners, homework routines, behavioral expectations—that have improved the families' dynamics. The program has had an empowering effect on participants. Many of the parents who went through the Parenting Journey have taken leadership roles within our school as class parents and PTA officers. Of equal importance are the changes we see in the students whose family members have participated in Parenting Journey. These children show greater focus, their behaviors are improved, and as a result, their academics have improved dramatically.

The student outcomes in one PS 503 classroom showed that reading scores were higher for those whose parents had taken Parenting Journey as compared with students whose parents had not.

Further studies will be made to test long-term effects on two generations of quality of life issues—family relations, school results, income levels, and well-being.

Acknowledgments

PARENTING JOURNEY WAS CONCEIVED AND CREATED BY many people: first of all, by the families themselves, who taught us what we needed to know to be able to be of service to them. They taught us to listen. While their names and details have been changed to protect their privacy, I will always be indebted to them and have fond lifelong memories of their faces, expressions, laughs, and sometimes outrageous language.

I am indebted to my two great mentors, David Kantor and Salvador Minuchin, without whose thinking and teaching we would still be milling around in old-fashioned notions of therapy think, and we might even be forbidden to laugh with our clients and at ourselves.

Cheryl Vines came to The Family Center shortly after it opened as our bookkeeper. Her children were little, and she lived nearby—a convenient job where she remained for 25 years, holding virtually every position in the organization, doing what needed to be done, from shoveling snow to becoming a first-class trainer, and eventually, executive director for 15 years. She was a major creator of group programs, and embodies the soul of the organization. She is a beloved friend and supporter of the mission.

Ann Marie Teuber arrived as an intern as we were transitioning from housing projects to a group format and has been the longest-running Parenting Journey group facilitator and trainer. Like Cheryl, the work is in her blood, and she has brought an element of spirituality and positivity that radiates throughout the organization. She has participated in creating all versions of Parenting Journey and has helped me by reading and critiquing every word of this book.

Rose Niles McCrary, a divinity school graduate student, ran our first program in the housing projects and was my "on the ground" thought partner and traveling companion throughout the first years.

There are many more on the staff who, at different times, enriched the program, devised interventions, and developed curricula, and became brilliant group facilitators and trainers. In our earliest days, Theresa Ormand taught me what it was like living in a housing development, and viscerally knew what would work and what wouldn't. Rob Guise, the pied piper carpenter, who was in training as a family therapist, whose truck (one of our first offices) was joyously followed by the children in the first children's groups; Adele D'Ari, relentless on the phone with timid families; Ariel Greenidge, who developed a domestic violence program; Marilyn Cook, who named Parenting Journey; Norman Beach, Rob Fladger, Jeanne Breeden, Sandra Brown, were among the first "team;" Dianne Zaccheo brought "special objects" to Parenting Journey; Matt Cibula brought the Soap Opera; Tricia Axsom ran the Family Choices program off-site; Diana Appel supervised the first group programs; Betty Farbman was the first administrator, doing everything that needed doing, while her baby boy was perched on the waiting room sofa. Since then, many administrative staff have held the organization together.

In building the group program, Delores Reyes was our guru on addictions and how to develop a program for recovering addicts. Amy Brinn was (and is) a brilliant clinician and trainer, as well as an insightful program developer. Carolina Grynbal, lead trainer and senior advisor, had enough wit, brilliance, energy, and commitment for five people. Cristina Pachano, our butterfly, and main developer of Parenting In America—making life joyful, and now its clinical director. Maude Laroche developed the Haitian Parenting In America. Thomas Haynes, who never knew he was a gifted teacher and counselor until recently, was a major developer of the men's program. Lyn Styczynski, a longtime member of the team, held positions of clinical director and senior supervisor. Karen Welling developed Transitions, a two-generation domestic violence program. Caroline Kistin designed and developed our evidence-based evaluation.

Many more who joined the tribe because they cared about the mission and wanted to give back contributed to developing Parenting Journey. With every discussion or supervision meeting, new ideas and new interventions were introduced.

My first real mentor, before the Family Center, but certainly the person most responsible for teaching me there was so much more to learn, was Hubie Jones, then, in the early 1970s, the executive director of The Roxbury Multi-Service Center. In his 90s, he is still an adored community leader.

And then there are friends who helped with the book.

Roz Zander—my painting partner, 43 years of dearest friendship, all-night discussions, and many bottles of wine; disagreeing, agreeing, creating her own therapeutic language and interventions, and ours, teaching me her ways of thinking about possibility, and helping me with the book. She was also an initial supervisor on the Family Center staff.

Jody Scheier, my dear friend from whom I learned action-oriented, experiential techniques over almost 50 years— my teacher, my friend, my collaborator. She has patiently read every word of this book at least twice and contributed invaluable advice, and is still a senior supervisor of staff.

Other friends were encouraging and helpful: the clinical knowledge of Dr. Richard Weissbourd, Katya Fels Smyth, Dr. Barry Zuckerman, Dr. Gerald Adler, Dr. Richard Chasin, Dr. Rick Reinkraut, and Thomas Haynes pushed me along, adding their wisdom and insights.

Deogratias Niyizonkiza, through an accidental meeting on a street corner, introduced me to Burundi, his native land, and asked me to help him deal with the terrible amount of PTSD in a country wracked by a 12-year war. There in his amazing holistic community, Village Health Works, we developed a version of Parenting Journey. The community members named this program "Opening Up," and it is from these beautiful souls that this book takes its name.

Margaret Blood, our champion in Guatemala, brought us to another unknown land and made us realize the international possibilities of a program focused on the common human condition.

My editorial saviors in this effort are David Chanoff, who enthusiastically took the text and put it in some order resembling a book; my dear friend of many years, writer Roger Rosenblatt, who believed I could do it, spiked it up, cut it down, and was a best friend when I needed him. I believe one could call it love. Bailey Georges, an experienced and sensitive editor, restructured the text, improving its readability, and made this manuscript into a real book. And thanks to Andrea Rosenberg for her technical assistance. Without all of these people, there would be no book. As we continue to develop and enter a new period, we have added the extraordinary talents and wisdom of Bern Haan, our board chair, and Bithiah Carter, treasurer and co-chair. And most critically in closing the process, I want to send a deep appreciation to my patient and wise agent, William Clark.

I am indebted to my partner, Martin Garbus, who was encouraging, patient, and tolerated my sometimes inattention to him with loving understanding.

Resources

TRAINING

IF YOU ARE INTERESTED IN TAKING ANY OF THE TRAININGS OFFERED by Parenting Journey, please log on to its website, Parentingjourney .org.

Trainings available: PJ 1 (Basic, introductory); PJ2 (continuation focusing more on the future than the past); Parenting in America (focusing on immigrants learning to assimilate two cultures, one they bring with them and another which their children are learning); Parents in Recovery (for parents struggling with addictions); PJ for Men; (especially for men, although men may take the other PJs as well); Transitions (for domestic violence survivors and their children ages 6–12).

PARENTING JOURNEY–RELATED RESOURCE MATERIAL
Family Therapy

Boszormenyi-Nagy, I., & Spark, G.M. (1973). *Invisible loyalties.* New York, NY: Brunner Maze Publishers.

Boyd-Franklin, N. (2000). *Reaching out in family therapy.* New York, NY: Guilford Press.

Imber-Black, E., Roberts, J., & Whiting, R. (Ed.) (1988). *Rituals in families and family therapy.* New York, NY: W.W. Norton & Company.

Kagan, R., & Schlosberg, S. (1989). *Families in perpetual crisis*. New York, NY: W.W. Norton & Company.

Kantor, D., & Lehr, W. (1977). *Inside the family*. San Francisco, CA: Jossey-Bass.

Madsen, W. (1999). *Collaborative therapy with multi-stressed families*. New York, NY: Guilford Press.

McGoldrick, M., Giordano, M., & Garcia-Preto, N. (2005). *Ethnicity and family therapy*. New York, NY: Guilford Press.

Minuchin, S. (1977). *Families and family therapy*. Cambridge, MA: Harvard University Press.

Minuchin, S., Minuchin, P., & Colapinto, J. (1998). *Working with families of the poor*. New York, NY: Guilford Press.

Minuchin, S., Montalvo, B., Bernard, G., Rosman, B., & Schumer, F. (1967). *Families of the slums*. New York, NY: Basic Books.

Napier, A., & Whitaker., C. (1988). *The family crucible: The intense experience of family therapy*. New York, NY: Harper Perennial

Satir, V. (1983). *Conjoint family therapy*. Palo Alto, CA: Science and Behavior Books, Inc.

Wilson, A. (1994). *Fences*. New York, NY: Penguin Books.

Attachment Theory
Bowlby, J. (1969). *Attachment and loss*. New York, NY: Basic Books.

Fraiberg, S. (1975). Ghosts in the nursery: A psychoanalytic approach to the problems of impaired infant-mother relationships. *Journal of American Academy of Child Psychiatry*, 14, Summer 1975.

Siegel, D. (2010). *Mindsight: The new science of personal transformation*. New York, NY: Random House.

Winnicott, D. W. (1991). *Playing and reality*. London, UK: Routledge.

Trauma
Briere, J. (1992). *Child abuse trauma – Theory and treatment of the lasting effects*. Sage Publications, Inc.

Herman, J. (1997). *Trauma and recovery*. New York, NY: Basic Books.

Menakem, R. (2017). *My grandmother's hands: Racialized trauma and the pathways to mending our hearts and bodies*. Las Vegas, NV: Central Recovery Press.

Van Der Kolk, B. (2014). *The body keeps the score*. New York, NY: Viking Press.

Wylie, M. S. (2004). *The limits of talk: Bessel van der Kolk wants to transform the treatment of trauma.* Psychotherapy Networker Magazine.

Mendelsohn, M., Lewis Herman, J., Schatzow, E., Coco, M., Kallivayalil, D., & Levitan, J. (2011). *The trauma recovery group – A guide for practitioners.* New York, NY: Guilford Press.

Resilience

Seligman, M. (2011). *Flourish.* New York, NY: Simon & Schuster.

Valiant, G. (2012). *Triumphs of experience: The men of the Harvard study.* Cambridge, MA: Belknap Press.

Weissbourd, R. (1996). *The vulnerable child.* Boston, MA: Addison-Wesley.

Zander, R. (2000). *The art of possibility.* Cambridge, MA: Harvard Business School Press.

Action-Oriented Therapies

Blatner, A. (1996). *Acting-In* (3rd ed.). New York, NY: Springer.

Blatner, A. (2000). *Foundations of psychodrama: History, drama, and practice* (4th ed.). New York, NY: Springer.

Boal, A. (1985). *Theatre of the oppressed.* Theatre Communications Group.

Dayton, T. (1994). *The drama within psychodrama and experiential therapy.* Deerfield Beach, FL: Health Communications, Inc.

Goldman, E. E., & Morrison, D. S. (1984). *Psychodrama: experience and process.* Dubuque, IA: Kendall Hunt Publishing.

Moreno, J. L. (1946/1980). *Psychodrama.* (Vol 1). (6th ed.). Beacon, NY: Beacon House.

Moreno, J. L. (1973). *The theatre of spontaneity* (3rd ed.). Beacon, NY: Beacon House.

Perls, F. (1951). *Gestalt therapy: Excitement and growth in the human personality.* Julian Press.

Perls, F. (1989). *The gestalt approach and eye witness to therapy.* Science and Behavior Books.

Sacks, J. M. (1974). *The letter: Group psychotherapy & psychodrama. 27, 84-190.*

Schwartz, R. (1995). *Internal family systems therapy.* New York, NY: Guilford Press.

Mindfulness/Self Compassion

Bennet-Golman, T. (2001). *Emotional alchemy: How the mind can heal the heart.* The River Press.

Brach, T. (2003). *Radical acceptance: Embracing your life with the heart of a buddha.* New York, NY: Bantam Press.

Brown, B. (2012). *Daring greatly: How the courage to be vulnerable transforms the way we live, love, parent, and lead.* New York, NY: Gotham Books.

Fosha, D., Siegel, D., & Solomon, M. (Eds.) (2009). *The healing power of emotion.* New York, NY: W.W. Norton & Company.

Germer, C. (2009). *The mindful path to self-compassion: Freeing yourself from destructive thoughts and emotions.* New York, NY: Guilford Press.

Child Development/Parenting

Berg, I. K. (1994). *Family-based services: A solution-focused approach.* New York, NY: W.W. Norton & Company.

Fraiberg, S. (2005). *Angels in the nursery: The intergenerational transmission of benevolent parental influences.* Wilder Foundation.

Fraiberg, S., & Brazelton, T. B. (1996). *The magic years: Understanding and handling the problems of early childhood.* New York, NY: Simon & Schuster.

Ginott, H. (1967). *Between parent and child.* New York, NY: Avon.

Gordon, M. (2019). *Roots of empathy.* New York, NY: The Experiment.

Siegel, D. J., & Hartzel, M. (2003). *Parenting from the inside out.* New York, NY: Penguin Group.

Communication

Berzoff, J. (Ed.). (2012). *Falling through the cracks: Psychodynamic practice with vulnerable and oppressed populations.* New York, NY: Columbia University Press.

Faber, A., & Mazlish, E. (1980). *How to talk so kids will listen and listen so kids will talk.* New York, NY: HarperCollins.

McKay, M., Davis, M., & Fanning, P. (1983). *Messages: The communication skills book*. Oakland, CA: New Harbinger Publications.

Stone, D., Patton, B., & Heen, S. (1999). *Difficult conversations: How to discuss what matters most*. New York, NY: Penguin Books

Walker, M., & Rosen, W. (Eds). (2004). *How connections heal; Stories from relational-cultural therapy*. New York, NY: Guilford Press.

Education

Gordon, M. (2009). *Roots of empathy*. New York, NY: The Experiment.

Nathan, L. (2017). *When grit isn't enough*. Boston, MA: Beacon Press.

Shanker, S. (2017). *Self-Reg*. New York, NY: Penguin Books.

Tough, P. (2012). *How children succeed*. Boston, MA: Houghton Mifflin Harcourt.

Racism And Socal Justice

Baldwin, J. (1962). *The fire next time*. New York, NY: Vintage Books.

Coates, T. (2015). *Between the world and me*. New York, NY: Spiegel & Grau.

Goodman, D. J. (2013) *Cultural competency for social justice: A framework for student, staff, faculty and organizational development*. Dianegoodman.com/free-materials

Hopps, J. G., Pinderhughes, E., & Shankar, R. (1995). *The power to care: Clinical practice effectiveness with overwhelmed clients*. Free Press.

Kendi, I. X. (2017) *Stamped from the beginning: The definitive history of racist ideas in America*. New York, NY: Bold Type Books.

Kendi, I. X. (2019). *How to be an antiracist*. New York, NY: Penguin Random House.

MacLeod, J. (1987). *Ain't no makin' it*. Boulder, CO: Westview Press, Inc.

Morrison, T. (1970). *The bluest eye*. New York, NY: Washington Square Press.

Vance, J.D. (2016). *Hillbilly elegy*. New York, NY: HarperCollins.

Wilkerson, I. (2020). *Caste: The origins of our discontents*. New York, NY: Random House.